THE DOCTOR'S WIFE

THE DOCTOR'S WIFE

Battling Mental Illness through Marriage and Motherhood

SAMANTHA CABRERA

Calla Press

Printed in the United States of America

ISBN 978-0-5782-9371-4 (print)
ISBN 978-0-5782-9372-1 (e-book)

Published by Calla Press

Texas

Subject Heading: CHRISTIAN LIVING/PERSONAL MEMOIRS

Unless otherwise stated, Scripture quotations are from the New International Version (NIV) Holy Bible, New International Version®, NIV® Copyright ©1973, 1978, 1984, 2011 by Biblica, Inc.® Used by permission. All rights reserved worldwide.

To my husband and children, who made me a grateful wife and mother. *Nunca sabrás lo tanto que te amo.*

Contents

Prologue

And the God of all grace, who called you to his eternal
glory in Christ, after you have suffered a little while, will himself
restore you and make you strong, firm and steadfast.
1 Peter 5:10

For two years of our now five-year marriage, I chose to fill my emptiness with sin. My fingers grasped wine cigars and a bottle of El Guitarron liquor, while my heart grasped anger and bitterness. I knew marriage would be difficult, but I didn't expect our marriage to be so full of broken things: broken plates, broken guitar stands, broken glass, broken hearts, broken spirits. Most days, it was too much for my breaking mind to handle; it would be for Omar, too.

Two years into our marriage, I was diagnosed with major depressive disorder and traits of borderline personality disorder. For the longest time, I would whisper to my husband that I was OK, but after he pulled the bottle of liquor from the drawer while his wedding ring clanked against it, he knew, and I knew it, too. I was not all right. This depression would resurface once our baby boy was born, something no one could have prepared me for as a new mother. I'd weep in the early hours of the morning to nurse my babe, and I could never have imagined my motherhood journey would begin this way.

My story traces my marriage and motherhood woes through my mental illness. I tell my story because I know there are others who don't have it all together and need that grace story to make room for them, too. We are sufferers of the mind, and we need someone to hear us, to give us hope when depression looms over us because we lost that darling babe, or because we're having recurrent marital problems, or because our children don't seem to love us all that much anymore, or because we have lost someone. You're not alone.

Maybe you have picked up this book to make room for the broken in you, the part that is so deeply paralyzed by anguish that it feels insurmountable at times. I get it. There is room for you here.

There is room in our house, in our day-to-day lives—in my messy kitchen, in my day-to-day life, because I am a wife and mother who does not have it all together.

The nature of our household is ordinary. Laundry loads pile in our closet like leaf stacks in autumn. Dishes run a muck in our kitchen farm sink. Toys litter our wooden floors. Our evenings typically end with dinner, baths, prayer, and bedtime. When we have open days, we enjoy being wrapped up in each other as a family. We love meandering the vintage shop down the street from us, full of antique finds like quilted blankets, prairie-style desks, blue-striped ceramic wear, doilies, and old butter churns, a place where everything has a story and was once ritually used in a home. We live simply, enjoying our children and striving to live holy lives.

And just like you, there is another side to this story. There is anguish. Pain. Mourning. There are untold woes deep inside you, and I pray that this story brings you hope through your despair.

The Gospels mention Calvary is right outside Jerusalem's walls; it was forbidden in Jewish tradition to bury someone in the city. And so, Jesus's last entry into the city would be to die a gruesome death right outside the city walls, a place known as Golgotha, the place of skulls.

Calvary is both a heart-wrenching word but also a glorious word, the place where the other side of my story lies. We see the inerrancy of Christ through this word, but we also see something else. According to the Merriam-Webster dictionary, the word calvary has two definitions:

1: an open-air representation of the crucifixion of Jesus
2: an experience of usually intense mental suffering

It was in the garden of Gethsemane where Jesus sweated beads of blood in agony before his crucifixion; he knew he would be crushed and abused before being nailed to the wood of Calvary.

He did so for you and for me. I do know that the Gospels are as real as the big brown eyes of my son that stare at me while he eats his Cheerios. I know that Jesus Christ died and suffered, so I didn't have to.

He suffered at Calvary for all of our brokenness. He endured the spikes of seven-inch nails torn through his pure and holy flesh in seconds for that knee-deep sin you turn to, for that perverse mind, for that sting cutting through your wrist, for that cuss word you spat at your husband, or, for that deep anguish inside you. Jesus Christ crucified is the embodiment of anguish—*an open-air representation of anguish*. This Jesus is near to us. This Jesus weeps with us. This Jesus suffers with us. He died for all the hidden and unknown calvaries.

I have a calvary deep inside, too. A calvary where I have mourned things I've done in my marriage and in motherhood. While I can groan about these things, I can also remember what calvary means—it's the place where Jesus died for the broken me, *for all of the broken in me*.

He died at Calvary, so I didn't have to die to my own calvary.

I hope my story reminds you that your harvest of peace can also lie amongst the place of skulls because God's harvest has a place for everyone to yield from.

Part One

BATTLING MENTAL ILLNESS IN MARRIAGE

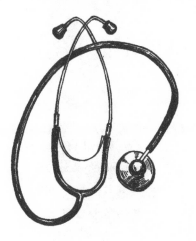

One

Undiagnosed

Is there no balm in Gilead?
Is there no physician there?
Why then, is there no healing
for the wound of my people?
Jeremiah 8:22

You know when you're driving down the dusty road, and the wheat field beside you becomes a long golden blur? Well, that's how our marriage was for the first couple of years; I know it was something holy in the making, but it all went by like a golden blur. I have finally taken the time to reflect on all that the Great Physician has done in my life; my story is not extraordinary, but it points to someone who is.

After being married to an OB-GYN for five years, I became as familiar with certain words as I am with *eggs* or *laundry*.

Words like *micrograms*, *blood*, *cc's*, *dilated*, *pushing*, *mom*, *baby*, *hysterectomy*, and so on. Then there are the less frequent words, like *cancer*, *no fetal pole*, or *dying*.

I've heard triumphant stories, and I've listened to sorrowful stories. Quite comical stories, too. While in residency, Omar had to deliver a patient who needed to have a bowel movement.

While my husband tried to tell her to come to the hospital bed because he knew the baby would debut any moment, she kept frantically shouting, "I need to poop! I need to poop!"

"Ma'am, I really need you to come back to the bed because I need to check you."

"Oh, I need to poop! I'm going to poop!"

"No, I really think you're going to have a baby!"

By this part of the story, my husband is chuckling. About one minute later, she had pooped on the corner of the suite floor. The patient still ended up with her sweet baby in her arms.

He had to deliver a baby with a terminal illness at a different time. Mom knew her baby would die just 24 hours after birth, but she still wanted to have a natural birth and wait as long as possible. Unfortunately, the baby's skull didn't form, a term called fetal acrania, and the brain was damaged by amniotic fluid, which is toxic to the nerves. It was this patient's fourth repeat c-section.

Whenever my husband comes home, I can tell by his face if it is a fallacious day or a disquieting one. Whenever he tells me a story of a patient who miscarried, I ask, "How is she doing,

Omar?" My heart breaks for the parents who will never witness their baby's nearness, smell their sweet breath, hear their giggles, or get to rock them to sleep. I don't quite understand how such loving and expectant parents have to endure such trauma and anguish.

Isn't it trauma that lingers in us only to come out of us in such unexpected ways? Doesn't the brokenness in all of us, in some way or another, accrue from anguish? There's trauma to the brain, yes. Trauma to organs. Trauma to an unborn baby, even. And then there's heart trauma, the kind of trauma that is like the trauma done to an unborn fetus, one can't see it outside of one's flesh, but it's there. Then something, painstakingly, unjustly, dies. In that dying, hope dies with it, and there is nothing but silence. Heart trauma is the most complex kind of trauma to heal from.

You won't know why you suddenly threw that silver spoon across the table and broke your husband's heart that night, but your trauma will know. Given time, your trauma will speak up eventually if it is not dealt with in a healthy way. It's a choice, though, to seek help and healing.

Like the choice was mine.

Trauma triggered me; it took me years to figure that out. One evening, Omar came home and had to take an urgent call.

"We'll need to do a transfer...." I remember his voice low in the closet. He returned to the room, and I couldn't wait to interrogate him.

"What happened?" I asked.

"A 21-weeker is going to lose her baby. The baby won't survive."

"Why won't the baby survive? You can't save it?"

"No, she's in labor, and she's going to be delivering the baby soon, and there's no way to stop it...she wants to be transferred, but you can't resuscitate a baby that is 21 weeks."

"That's probably because she wants someone to save her baby! You can save it! How do you know it'll die?"

"Because I know, my love. A baby that early will not survive."

"But how do you *know*?"

"Because the baby is too premature, my love." He heaved and sat on the bed.

"Yea, but how do you *really* know this baby can't survive? You're just going to give up on it? This poor mom just wants her baby to live, and she believes there's hope. That's why she's holding out! You're not even going to try?"

"There's nothing I can do, Samantha."

"There's always something someone can do. You could be that doctor that doesn't give up. Go and save her baby!"

By now, I was yelling, not quite sure why. Omar came to me then, seeing my tears.

"My love," he cupped my face. "Why are you taking this so personally? Is it because you think someone gave up on you?"

I wept in his arms and apologized for being adamant that he try to save a baby he knew was already dying. It turns out that the next day, the patient delivered her lifeless baby—the arm was purple because it had clotted off during labor. I cried. The doctor was right.

I often anguish for people I've never met, thinking of their sorrow after losing a baby. What do their days look like right after they find out?

*We'd need to do a repeat ultrasound...failed pregnancy...the betas are not rising... there's a baby without a heartbeat...*I overhear my husband on the phone with a patient, his voice calm. My heart tightens for this woman I've never met; the doctor relays the options: *pass pregnancy on your own...medication...D&C.*

In other patients, my husband is not quite sure where the pregnancy is being formed because while it usually grows in the uterus, it can also grow outside of it in what's called an ectopic pregnancy. Until it's determined where the pregnancy is, it's called a pregnancy of unknown location.

I think about the words *unknown location*. Isn't this sort of how we can define trauma? I can't quite pinpoint it, but I know it's there.

When Omar and I married in May 2017, we didn't know our imminent journey or what waited for us past the wedding threshold, but I did know the love he held like a newborn baby, so delicate and *graceful*, would slowly bring healing. His love is not my cure, only Christ's love is, but how my husband loved me changed my life.

However, it would be a long and heart-breaking journey before I would be brought up from this pain and, even more so, acknowledge it. I would turn to substances instead of Christ to fill my void. I would turn to the temporal things—*wine, cigars, and self-destructive behaviors.*

And yet, this is the story of my life. I am always inherently met with grace every time, and I don't deserve it. I only know to live my one life grateful and holy and to share this grace with others.

Our marriage would be the purification process I needed. Just like we chose an unbuilt wedding venue that looked like the scaffolding of Noah's ark, we would entrust the Lord with our new marriage. Would we be patient with one another through the *unbuilt* to witness how God builds us up together?

I know I'm a broken sinner. My hands are often battling the broken things, like my ceramic statues, my husband's music stand, or the vase full of white roses he picked for me from our greening garden. I can still see the water-stained carpet with broken glass and loosened petals.

I believe so many of us dealing with mental illness feel like there will be a day when we're suddenly *unbroken.* That our minds will somehow be *fixed* as though we're shiny mechanical robots awaiting the perfect nuts and bolts. They will never come. When God restores his creation and people, what was broken will then be made *whole.*

Take my twin sister as a prime example; she suffers from two rare diseases, Devic's disease, also called neuromyelitis optica (NMO), as well as avascular necrosis.

NMO has left her partially blind in one eye and her schedule full of bi-monthly infusions for the rest of her life. It is an immunological disorder that attacks the spinal cord and optic nerves. Apart from this, she suffers bone death in her right shoulder. The odds of her getting the perfect *nuts and bolts* are highly likely for a shoulder replacement.

While I pray with everything in me that her suffering does not make her heart hardened, I empathize with her pain. As her sister, while I desperately pray her pain away, I pray for her battered and broken heart even more.

I've seen first-hand what deep physical pain can do to some-one; "A joyful heart is good medicine, but a crushed spirit dries up the bones" (Prov. 17:22). I've seen my twin in good spirits, but I have seen her crushed so many times from the calamities of life. My heart anguishes for her. Still, you will often hear her laughter and her praise. The Lord will be glorified, and it is so in her story; her bone grafting surgery is a reminder of how God *grafts* us into the original tree so we can become par-takers of the nourishing root (Rom. 11:17). We weren't designed to live life *unbroken;* we were created to live *in* Christ *amidst* our brokenness so that his good grace would fill our holes. "Be gracious to me, O Lord, for I am languishing; heal me, O Lord, for my bones are troubled" (Psalm 6:2 ESV).

We were designed to live a Christ-exalting life in a Christ-denying world. This is mentioned in many different ways for the same reason because it's the only way we can depend on Christ. We are a broken people in a broken world striving to live holy for Christ Jesus.

Take it from someone who has scars on her body and all across her mind, nothing will make you feel *whole again* unless you rest, *completely and wholly broken, every bit of you*, in God alone. While medicine may help in not focusing on your scattered mood or your pain, it is not a cure-all. It's leverage.

So often, I would get flustered with my husband because he wouldn't understand what *I wanted*. I didn't want another righteous prayer spilled over me with hot breath. I needed *medicine*.

"How can I go to God in this when I can't even think straight? I need medicine to reach Him! I can't get through this stupid fog!" I yelled in agony one night. "I just can't do it anymore. I can't. I feel so alone in my thoughts that it's killing me."

The moonlight shone through the window, hitting my wedding ring; I saw the doctor's hand cover my own. "You're not alone," he whispered. "God has not left you. I will do my best to help you, my love."

My one and only husband could not love me out of my broken mess; it would take the exuding love of God at work *in and through* my husband to help me. Omar is not perfect, but he has always had a willing heart.

I remember when my episodes started becoming more gradual. I was checking out at the gas station, a cigar pack in my hands. I parked on the curbside under the shade of a tree and lit a cigar.

What is going on with me?

I puffed till the soot fell on my lap. The air conditioning was blowing in my hot face. People were walking to and from the shops with their bags, looking content under the midsummer sun. I numbly finished the cigar and cast it off like a fisher's net.

Meanwhile, my husband never knew. He never knew my secrets during the daytime.

At this point in my story, my depression was undiagnosed and untreated. While this secrecy consumed me, my phrenic activity did too.

Mental illness is a sick mind just like one has a sick bone; it needs treatment, or it, too, can cause demise. An abstract from *Medical Hypothesis* by E. Van Winkle states:

> During periodic detoxification crises, excess norepineph-rine floods synapses, overexcite postsynaptic neurons, and cause[s] symptoms ranging from mild anxiety to violent behavior....depression returns....Recovery is a detoxification process and can be facilitated by therapy that involves re-experiencing childhood traumas, releasing, and redirecting repressed emotions.[1]

Winkle stated how suppression of emotions could cause depression in many cases; those who have come from trauma, particularly those who have suppressed their feelings, could have violent episodes or behavior later on.

And so was the case with me.

If your one broken mind feels like it's on its death bed, like mine often does, God can *graft* it into his sacred ground, where peace abounds. It doesn't mean we'll always be at peace, but we'll always be grafted to the Christ of peace; when we're feeling like a dying shoot, he comes up and springs forward a warmth of peace from the *nourishing root*.

When this happens, all I can do is give thanks because I am always gently reminded that he is ever with me, holding me up. He is with us through the sickness—through the process of *healing*. Even when I feel despondent, alone, detached, or deeply troubled, there is my Father whose harvest never runs out, and my Father with arms ever-extending toward me.

I desperately needed to address the wounding of my soul and mind, not just with a doctor but with my Great Physician. I needed to bandage my open wounds with the *Balm of Gilead*, but little did I know that it would be my very doctor-husband to help me do this. Just like a bone grafting surgery, though, there is always a great deal of pain before the inner healing takes place.

Two

In Sickness and In Health

*And the word [sumpatheó] is a deep word, signifying to suffer
with us until we are relieved. And this affection, thus stirred up,
is it which moves him so cordially to help us.*
Thomas Goodwin, *The Heart of Christ in Heaven Towards
Sinners on Earth*

Those who belittle the sickness of the mind may have
never themselves suffered from it. This is why sharing
our stories is vital to the heart of sufferers. It's comforting to
let someone pull up close to you and whisper *I get it, and I'm
here with you in it.*

In 2019, I was diagnosed by my psychiatrist with major depressive disorder (MDD) and traits of borderline personality
disorder (BPD).

I remember the time I had completely lost it after a pop-up

sale at a market event. We had just finished my display show-casing my paintings. All was well until we arrived home, and I started packing things away. My husband came in carrying my work.

"Perhaps you should think about getting another job, and then you can run your business on the side," he said rather nonchalantly.

Bent down with my hair in my face, I felt like I had been slapped on the cheek. I stood slowly and looked at him, sorrow deep in my eyes.

In other words, you suck. You're stupid. You're never going to grow your business. It's wasting my *money.* The snake of the garden hissed in my ear, and there was no unhearing it.

"Excuse me?" I asked. In a moment, my surprise turned to rage.

"My love, I'm just saying—"

"I know what you're saying." An obscenity slipped through my mouth. "I'm wasting your money, is that it? I suck, right? I'm just wasting my time, right? This is all meaningless, RIGHT?" The rage slipped into me like a worm slipping into fruit to devour it.

"This art thing is stupid, right?"

I stormed into my painting room, anger burning my fingers, my throat, *all of me.*

"Then what's the point of all of this?" I yelled. I threw my paintbrushes onto the floor; I thrust everything onto the carpet in a mad tirade.

"What's the point of this scanner then—what!?" I grabbed

the two-hundred-dollar scanner and harshly thrust it to the floor. I heard cracks as it thudded near his feet, unrepairable. That was the scanner my husband had gifted me; I remember being so giddy as I slipped off the wrapping and kissed him. *Thank you for believing in me, my love.*

I grabbed the nearest lamp and smashed it against the wall; the light broke apart and spilled dark. I yelled at him all the horrible things before telling him I was running away for good.

"Stop it! Or, I'm going to call the cops on you," my husband shouted as he tried to gather me in his arms.

"Call them. I don't give a crap! I'd rather go to jail than live with you," I cried and tried to fight him. I tried to escape. I wept loudly in his arms, so loudly I'm surprised we never did see the cops through our windows. At one point, he tried to cover my mouth.

"Never *ever* lay a hand on me again," I shouted.

He apologized for trying to quiet me the wrong way. He was scared of others hearing us, while I was scared of not being enough, of never measuring up.

My anger turned to deep remorse. I knew what I had done and what I could not *undo*. The scanner that we had waited months for was now broken. I cried because I knew how much this hurt him. How could I be so in love with my husband and then be the one to hurt his heart the most?

"I'm horrible. I'm just a horrible, disgusting person, Omar. Why don't you leave me?" I cried into his soft, warm arm. "I give you permission."

He laughed softly.

"I'm not leaving you, my love. I'm never leaving you," he said into my hair as he kissed my head. This love was the prescription my heart needed. I was somehow met with tenderness in the midst of my unspoken pain and anger. Why? How? How could anyone love me over this frightening mess? Wouldn't anyone else just leave me?

Probably.

However, at the beginning of our marriage, my husband didn't know how to manage my pain; he tried to medicate it with his own strength, but that proved wrong. Over time, he started to meet my episodes with *tender grace,* and it never failed to stop me in my bullish episodes. I was not familiar with seeing grace poured out after wrath.

During my rages, I always felt inferior or rejected, and behind the anger on my lips lay sorrow. My husband would grasp my shoulder, "What are you so insecure about, my love?" His brown eyes would search me, search me like no one ever has, and for the life of me, I didn't have a single answer

"I feel rejected like no one truly cares about me. Unloved," I whispered as tears stung my eyes.

"I love you," he said.

I started weeping in my husband's arms. I needed healing. I needed someone to look good and hard at my pain, something no one had ever done in my entire life. Isn't this where Christ would meet me? In the *violence* and *conflict?* Could this not be evermore true to my broken spirit? Through this painful wilderness, God would whisper tenderly into my hair: *Beloved, come home. Come home to where you belong. Come home broken. Come home pained, and I am here for all of you.*

My breath would catch in my throat, my eyes clenched, and I'd start weeping until good reminders flooded me, reminding me that I am deeply loved by an all-knowing Father. Jesus walked into my dark mess and came up to everything that was dead in me to liven it all.

"You are my greatest ministry," my husband whispered into my hair. He always reminded me that over his profession, over his daily grind, over his own service, I was his greatest ministry. My husband sacrificially loves me in a way most will never see, but I get to witness his love for me every day, the kind of love that truly embodies the love of Christ.

While my husband is a broken sinner like me, fighting his own battles, he still loved me through it all. In Christ's sanctifying love, I'm able to meet my husband *in that same love.* Not the scraps of love I think I have left to give but love from the harvest before me, the love from God's bountiful harvest.

> Though the fig tree does not bud
> and there are no grapes on the vines,
> though the olive crop fails
> and the fields produce no food,
> though there are no sheep in the pen
> and no cattle in the stalls,
> yet I will rejoice in the Lord,
> I will be joyful in God my Savior. (Hab. 3:17-18)

Even when I feel like I have nothing left to give in this marriage, I can glean from Christ's strength; I can pull from his harvest when I have none of my own. I can glean from his harvest even when I fail my husband with the spewing of hurtful words.

The moments I yelled hurtful things, I was usually frustrated and annoyed at my husband's constant correction, something he has worked on and humbled himself in. He still doesn't get it right, but it's not as recurring as it once was. At one point, I snapped.

"I'm sick of you telling me how much I'm doing wrong. I'm tired of you living like a saint. I'm tired of you thinking you're the most righteous person in the world. Because you're the doctor, and you're always right, right? Forget what we, common folk, have to say! I'm sick of it!" I yelled.

"My love, that's not what I'm doing. Please come back," he said as I gathered my book bag to head out the door.

"You know what, Omar, I'm going to buy you a big freakin' horse so you can get on and get over it," I yelled.

"That's not how the saying goes—" he shot back. "You want me to get off my high horse."

I tried to hold my laughter as my hand reached for the doorknob, my bag falling towards my wrist.

"You and your made-up sayings," he chuckled as he put his arms around me, dropping my bag. I could not help but smile. I did not want to smile during these moments, but it happened quite a bit.

"No, I'm really upset with you. I'm not smiling right now," I smirked.

"My sweet love, I'm *for* you. We're a team. Please don't think these things of me," he stroked my face with his hands. I let a big breath out and put my head on his shoulder.

"I'm sorry," I whispered.

"I forgive you," he said.

His tender grace met my anger; my tender husband somehow calmed my rage. Perhaps God used humor to calm me down because he knows I love a good laugh; in either case, it always worked. "Grace has a grand laughter in it," Marilynne Robinson once wrote. [2]

I whispered into my husband's cheek that night, *thank you for loving me through this—all of this.* My hands met his face, and he grinned. My God would meet me in the *breaking of myself* to remind me that I don't need to *break things* to feel *whole in my brokenness.*

I'd be numb after drinking tequila in hiding, rummaging for a blanket to hide it in. I'd be sick to my stomach after smoking cigars, feeling like I belonged at the bottom of the sea. Yet, God sent me someone who wouldn't be scared of my kind of broken. God sent me a man he knew I *needed*, someone that would help me see the broken in me is part of the main surgery of my life to give me a new body (Phil. 3:21).

We are always on the table, exposed under the Surgeon's hands. This is good news. We are God's hardest cases, yet he never once takes his gloves off, gives up, or scrubs off.

God daily bears our burdens (Psalm 68:19). He is perfecting

the good work in us every single day (Phil. 1:6). He enjoys being the bringer of healing and healing our diseases (Psalm 103:3).

I'm often reminded of the bleeding woman, especially given that I hear many stories of *bleeding, hemorrhaging, abdominal trauma,* and so forth.

And a woman was there who had been subject to bleeding for twelve years, but no one could heal her. She came up behind him and touched the edge of his cloak, and immediately her bleeding stopped.

"Who touched me?" Jesus asked.

When they all denied it, Peter said, "Master, the people are crowding and pressing against you."

But Jesus said, "Someone touched me; I know that power has gone out from me."

Then the woman, seeing that she could not go unnoticed, came trembling and fell at his feet. In the presence of all the people, she told why she had touched him and how she had been instantly healed. Then he said to her, "Daughter, your faith has healed you. Go in peace." (Luke 8:43-48)

I wonder how our Third Gospel writer, Luke, a physician, felt when he discovered this. Knowing this poor woman spent all her money on doctors, not one physician could heal her. After twelve years, can you imagine how she felt? Can you imagine the anguish she felt?

My husband has had many cases of bleeding. Of course, we have come far in the medical analysis of bleeding cases, so it's not difficult to assess what's causing the bleeding and how to fix it. However, doctors do not have all the answers; they can't prevent cancer from happening if it's God's will any more than they can prevent a fetus from dying. God's will prevails.

Still, this woman believed in doctors for twelve years before she saw the Savior of the world; it just took one look at him, and she knew this man was the Messiah. Afraid and ashamed, she came from behind Jesus to touch his cloak. The story could have been very different if Luke and the apostles had witnessed this woman pushing through the crowd to get to Jesus, probably calling out, "Jesus! Help me! I've been bleeding for twelve years, and no one can help me!"

It's a very different story when we throw tantrums and beg God to heal us, to move on our behalf. It would also be different if we never went up to Jesus to begin with. Instead, this suffering woman did none of this. She didn't even want Jesus to see her face, but she knew by faith that Jesus Christ would heal her. To suffer as she did is to be brought so low that you can't even stand burdening someone else even though this is what God came for wrapped as a baby, for the suffering, the sinners, the broken, and for you. For those ailing of the body and ailing of the mind, and for those mental calvaries.

This healing is a process that takes holy work, something only God can do. While medicine may be a gateway to stable moods, it is not the healer here. My husband is not the healer here. My house, my job, my work, my daily striving, my friends, and my church are not the healers. They are aids to healing, but God does it. Our Great Physician does true healing.

"As much as I want to change you, I can't. That's something only God can do," Omar would whisper. As much as it hurt, it's true. I realized that without repentant love, there is no right love. Without putting all of my trust into God's healing and ways, which is always putting myself last, there would be no changing, no growing up out of this pain.

When I went to my husband with my pain, it turned into wrath, but when I met God first, it always changed the story. It feels like a thousand times I have run straight into Omar with my pain, and I have easily slipped past the God I love, the God I say I follow, obey, and worship. Instead, Omar gets the brunt of my offenses.

Pain and healing are like prickly gooseberries; the healing process may be painful exteriorly, but the healing is sweet once inside. It takes time to get there, though. One can't just throw the whole prickly gooseberry in one's mouth. God, in his omniscience, formed a man he knew would help me become more purified. This is a promise within marriage. It is both holy and troubling, a painful purification, a tender dichotomy of suffering and love. This is why I'm sharing my table, *gooseberries and all*, with you to remind you that you are not alone. Your mental health matters. There is no broken part of you for which Jesus Christ did not break on the cross. If we come to him in all our anguish, he will surely be with us. Emmanuel.

God's marital sanctification process is now something I cling to. Even though it's painful, it's a purging that must take place for us to become more of the Christ-bearers we are called to be. Again, God often uses pain to heal and pained people to bring about his purposes.

> For just as we share abundantly in the sufferings of Christ, so also our comfort abounds through Christ. If we are distressed, it is for your comfort and salvation; if we are comforted, it is for your comfort, which produces in you patient endurance of the same sufferings we suffer. And our hope for you is firm, because we know that just as you share in our sufferings, so also you share in our comfort.... We were under great pressure, far beyond our ability to endure, so that we despaired of life itself. Indeed, we felt we had received the sentence of death. But this happened that we might not rely on ourselves but on God, who raises the dead. (2 Cor. 1:5-7,9)

Just as Paul's prison arrests weren't because he was doing something lawfully wrong, but because he was obedient to his calling, so it is with us. Sufferings will happen whether or not we are obedient, but true obedience always yields the harvest.

Moses had a speech disorder and led the Israelites out of Egypt. God kind of had to thump him on the head, though. King Saul likely had Bipolar Disorder I [3] and died by his own sword. Now, we know what not to do and how pride and self-absorption can consume you. The Holy Bible is suffused with stories where people disobey God, and we see the repercussions; for one, we can't expect God to bring healing to our brokenness if we keep disobeying him.

In his own doing and in fear, Saul disobeyed God. He missed the mark, and because of it, he missed out on the blessing and took his life.

"What have you done?" asked Samuel. Saul replied, "When I saw that the men were scattering, and that you did not come at the set time, and that the Philistines were assembling at Mikmash, I thought, 'Now the Philistines will come down against me at Gilgal, and I have not sought the Lord's favor.' So I felt compelled to offer the burnt offering."

"You have done a foolish thing," Samuel said. "You have not kept the command the Lord your God gave you; if you had, he would have established your kingdom over Israel for all time. But now your kingdom will not endure; the Lord has sought out a man after his own heart and appointed him ruler of his people, because you have not kept the Lord's command." (1 Samuel 13:11-14)

I had an awful habit of blaming Omar for all of my outbursts. Like Saul seemed to blame everyone but himself, I did the same. "It's you! It's you! Because you said this—" when the facts may be straight, but the blame falls on me for lashing out.

My reaction is my responsibility. My husband didn't tell me to throw a lamp or a glass vase. I needed to acknowledge that though I was in pain, though I was hurt, the little kingdom I'd built on justifying my pain needed to crumble. In the end, our pain matters to Jesus. It's not going to be effective if we're yelling across the room versus being humble like the bleeding woman.

Jesus Christ is near the broken-hearted, and he is the one who can relate most to our pain. The point is, there is no mental illness unknown to God; there is no part of you unseen and unknown by him. There is no painful, scarring part of your life that God has not already filtered through his just hands; he's using it for his glory and for your utmost good.

Three

My Brokenness

*No woman who has not learned to master herself can be
trusted to submit willingly to her husband. And that word
willingly means that she does not merely resign herself to something she cannot avoid. It means that by an act of her own will,
she gives herself.*
Elisabeth Elliot, *Let Me Be a Woman*

I remember walking the corridors in Mexico as a young girl
of seven. Looking at the shops, the crumbling foundations
of fading salmon-pink mortar, the dangling Mexican dolls
from the ends of sale carts held by older men with white hair, I
felt my eyes drawn to someone. Almost naked, save for a small
maroon wrap, a woman sat outside the entrance of a Carne
shop, breastfeeding her child. This woman's long black hair
wrapped gently around her baby and bare shoulders. I didn't

flinch as I stared at her, and then I willed myself to go before her and held out my five dollars. She hesitated at first, then smiling, she took the money and glanced down at her baby. I walked away feeling empty for her, even as a small girl with the world in her hands.

As a seven-year-old little girl, I didn't realize that in studying her, I had been looking at myself as an adult woman, sitting lowly against a wall, exposed, full of hopelessness, and longing for someone to look my way.

When I got married, I still felt like this woman against the wall, ignored and desperate. Again, with no actual diagnosis, my depression worsened over time. My episodes happened so frequently that my hope was falling as leaves do in autumn, my heart bare and uncovered for what would come.

I can remember running to the bathroom, pinning up my black hair. I quickly brushed my teeth, put a new layer of matte lipstick on, and lit some vanilla candles in the house. I didn't want to tell my husband what I had done.

"Why did you marry me?" I whispered, feeling the anguish within me begin to swell when he arrived.

"Because I love you," he smiled, still holding my face. Oh, these words. If I could only let my pain rest there and not wallow in the misfortune of my broken sins.

"But I'm not good for you, Omar," I said, looking into his eyes. The vanilla candles flickered, and Omar blew out one beside us on the table. Smoke rose and pooled in the air.

"Don't say that, my love. You're the only person for me," he said. I fell into his lap and wept, smelling the lingering burnt vanilla scent. But why did Omar have to marry someone like me? He could have anyone else more sophisticated, less troubled, and more normal.

Before Omar got home, I was at the gas station getting the forbidden apple. I slipped the cigar pack into my tawny purse and drove home, my mind running away. The sunlight spilled into my car, landing on my sunken, defeated face. I had seen him talking to another woman at the hospital, and it instantly planted an evil root in me that grows deep and takes an exca-vator to uproot. He asked me how I was when he got home.

"Good," I replied. My pinned hair fell to my shoulders, and I sighed in annoyance.

"Why are you being like this?" he asked with his brown eyes squinting.

"I saw you earlier talking to another woman. How's that? Is that what you wanted to hear?" I leered at him, both anger and betrayal breaking me apart.

"My love, whatever you saw, it was nothing. You have to trust me," he would utter with assurance in his voice. This word, *trust*, oh, how achingly hard it was to do at that moment.

"Well, guess what? I don't trust you," I found my voice domineering. Past pains of rejection sprung to my mind; I heard the verbal abuse, felt the mental abuse, and felt the abandonment.

"I'm just not good enough for you, am I?" I yelled while tears filled my eyes. He begged me to stop. I didn't listen. I carried the anguish in my arms while I gathered my bag, half my rack of clothes, toiletries, and phone charger, and stormed out of our apartment.

This is something I would do on a chronic basis.

"Find someone else to marry," I said as I slammed our front door. I shoved everything into my car and sped off. My knuckles clenched; fingers tight.

I drove to the same parking lot. *That's right, keep running. He doesn't care about you. He admires and wishes he had other, more sophisticated women than you. Less troubled and stupid women than you.* The lies seemed so real that I cried myself tired. My throat would twinge as I'd try to speak out to God. *I don't think I can do this much longer, Lord.* With my elbows propped on my steering wheel, my shaky fingers ran up and down my face. *What is my marriage if it looks like this?*

I didn't want our marriage to look like this. I didn't want our marriage to suffer. I didn't care about winning or losing. I just loved him enough. I imagined him at home alone, bent over in prayer. Omar would tell me within time how he'd cry when I'd leave, his shoulders shuddering in tears and torment, crying out, *God, why did you give me a suffering marriage?* I can imagine my one and only husband breaking apart, wondering why, on this hellish night, he had to suffer so. He would later tell me that he'd begin praying for me. *Father, don't let her do anything that would hurt herself. May she realize your love for her. May she listen to you, Lord. Heal her heart, God.*

I ended up driving home, feeling like my soul had been beaten but was cradled at night in the loving arms of my husband, my mind falling asleep to prayers.

The next morning wasn't any more graceful. One would think a new morning lavished with God's new mercies and grace would be better, but it wasn't. No one knew my nightly tears except my husband. It all became so unbearable. I became bitter, frustrated, and angry; sadly, my husband didn't enjoy coming home.

Later on that same day, I would visit the hospital to have lunch with Omar. As we said goodbye again, the bitterness took over.

"I'll see you after work," Omar said as he kissed me gently on the lips at the hospital entrance. I walked away, insecurity lurking within me like a lion, and as I drove off, I saw him talking to another blonde-haired woman. It was nothing, of course, but everything was iridescently wrong to me. After I saw that, I drove to the grocery store. I shook it off, whatever gross feeling came over me, and walked in. I already had a scribbled list. I walked the aisles, gathering what we needed. I picked up the milk, the bread, and the eggs, meandered a bit, and then passed it. *Don't.* I felt my hands reach out and take it. I stuffed it into my red shopping cart and hurried to the speedy checkout line. I gave her my ID and rushed to my car. I drove home with a heavy heart, the guilt already creeping in. I parked my car, entered our apartment, and started crying. I knelt on the floor and wept. It was only 3:30 p.m.

I got up and stashed the liquor in a drawer. I went about cleaning to hide any evidence of suspicion, feeling horrible and yet thrilled that something would finally make me feel something and calm my anxieties.

It was only half an hour before my husband came home that I would unscrew the gold lid and drink straight from the bottle. It was a nice burn down my throat, and as cliché as it sounds, I did gulp it down like lemonade on a summer's day.

My husband came home, and we got into an argument. It usually started with him doing something that would offend me, and thus, a wailing storm would begin. It never had to do with the very sin I was hiding, the very sin that would break me more.

"What are you hiding from me?" I asked dejectedly.

"I'm not hiding anything, my love," Omar said as he placed his backpack on the table. The daily mental agony that I was in would not let me believe this. He never wants to come home. He always seems to be thinking about something else. He's always going to his prayer closet.

"Well?" I fumed. "Are you going to finally be honest with me and tell me what you're hiding from me?" Tears welled in my eyes.

"You need help, my love. I'm serious. We need marriage counseling, and you need therapy. You need a lot of heal—"

"I don't need anything. I'm leaving you. I don't need you, and you clearly want to go and be with someone else."

"My love, why do you keep saying that? I want you. I want you to be free—"

"I am free. Who knew marrying you I'd feel like I'm in the deepest pit of hell I've ever been in!" I wailed again, the feelings overtaking me. "I'm not loved. No one cares about me. No one cares if I lived or died. I hate life! I hate living...." I sobbed, and without thinking, I grabbed his guitar stand and smashed it against the window. I broke a blind.

"You're crazy! Ingrate!" my husband shouted.

"You hate me! You don't love me. You're a liar. You're cheating on me! You want me to leave? I'll leave," my blood vessels pulsed hard in my neck while obscenities slipped through my lips. I rushed to the kitchen and grabbed a knife.

"I can't do it anymore. I can't—" I wailed. My husband rushed to me.

"Stop it, my love. Put the knife down," he gently said as he tried to take the knife from my hands. I gave up and melted. I sobbed on the kitchen floor.

"Nobody wants me," I yelled. "Nobody cares if I lived or died. They only care about you. You're the important one!"

"That's not true, my love," he smiled as he strongly took my face in his hands. "You are loved. I love you. I love you, Samantha. Don't listen to those lies..." he breathed into my face.

I yelled for him to get off and ran out of the house barefoot. I walked on the hot cement and sat under a large tree. I remember the thousands of oak leaves and how they swayed and flickered in the sunlight.

God, please speak to me. Please help me through this mental agony. I swept my hands into my hair, pulled the strays away from my face, and breathed in and out again. The cool breeze swept over me.

At this moment, I felt God speak to me. He met me here in my anguish. I felt the softness of who he was meet me when I ran away. He was there. He would reveal that this is not the end. This would not be the end, not of me nor our marriage. I was sitting in a parking lot. I had to go back home.

Do I stay in my pain on this cement, or do I surrender all of me in this moment of mine to the one who bled for me? Giving glory to Jesus is choosing to do the Christ-exalting thing in the midst of being so wrapped up in myself and my own pain. It's, as Elisabeth Elliot wrote, *the mastering.*

Romans 12:2 states, "Do not conform to the pattern of this world, but be transformed by the renewing of your mind. Then you will be able to test and approve what God's will is—his good, pleasing and perfect will." In order to not conform, we must choose not to conform.

The choice was mine, not my husband's.

Do you want to be a part of my glory today, beloved? I felt his cool whisper in my soul as hot tears spilled on my kneecaps. *I want to ever be a part of your glory story, Father.*

I didn't know what to expect when I walked in. I didn't know if Omar would be gone, and he was annoyed with me, I didn't know. I walked in. He was on the couch, praying, keeled over like a little boy. He looked up, his eyes were red-brimmed.

"I'm sorry," I started crying and went to him. He opened his arms, and I laid my head on his lap and cried. "I'm a horrible person. I'm a failure."

"You're not a horrible person. You're not a failure. I love you, Samantha," he said and picked me up, "I love you. I'm not going anywhere. You need to stop listening to Satan's lies. You need to," he said with his brows raised. I nodded, not knowing how to do that, and embraced him, not wanting to let go. I loved this man more than he would ever know. And still, I'd hurt this man more than he would ever know, and still, the grace bestowed. *Don't listen to the lies. You are so loved, my love.*

My doctor-husband's prayers were like his prescriptions for my sick heart. As we lay in bed, I whispered to my husband if he could pray over us. He stroked my face, looking deeply into me.

Father, we come to you as broken sinners in need of your grace. I come before you, Lord, as a husband of a hurting wife. I ask, Lord, that you give her peace in her pain, joy in her journey. Give her strength when she's alone to fight the battle of her mind. Even tonight, Lord, speak to her heart of your love for her. May you be all she desires, and may she always desire to be holy before you, Lord. We pray in Christ's name. Amen.

He wiped the tears away from my sulky face as we turned back in bed. We could hear the crickets' praises and the frog's high-pitched whirring. It somehow lulled me to sleep, and I felt the wooing of my soul towards an everlasting Father.

My husband's reflection of Christ's love still brings me healing. His posture in our marriage is humble, nurturing, and romantic. God, in his infinite wisdom and grace, blessed me with someone whose traits would slowly bring me healing. While he is not perfect in many ways and will continue to fail me at times, we are gracefully woven. I would later come to know that he coveted women's beauty, but he graciously willed himself to be vulnerable. This is what he was hiding from me. I was grateful that we have a marriage where we are open in our struggles, in our own brokenness, and bring things into the light. James 5:16 says: "Therefore confess your sins to each other and pray for each other so that you may be healed. The prayer of a righteous person is powerful and effective."

There is no righteousness apart from Christ. My husband is not the master of righteousness, nor am I. My husband is a wretched sinner just as I am; his stature is meaningless unless for the glory of God, as is mine. A lot of my striving to get better was hard for Omar to see at times. If I had another episode, he would retract into a derogatory comment that I'm starting back at square one, which always broke me. In one of my favorite books, *Gilead*, Marilynne Robinson said my feelings best: "These people who can see right through you never quite do you justice because they never give you credit for the effort you're making to be better than you are, which is difficult and well meant and deserving of some little notice." So, while I understand my husband's frustrations with me at progress, the progress must be nurtured, not discounted. If little progress is nurtured well, it makes room for much more.

God simply won't give up on you and is rooting for your progress, too. Even if you are terminally ill, chronically sick, mentally unstable, divorced, scarred, or ineptly broken, God is near you and wants to root for you.

I remember when my husband had a patient with a poor prognosis. Her bag of water had broken at 19 weeks; one of his partners had admitted the patient and made the plan to induce her after thoroughly counseling her about the grave risks for the baby should she remain pregnant. The great risks included: the baby could pass away in the uterus or after delivery, she could deliver a very premature baby with a high chance of disabilities, and/or she could possibly end up developing an infection in her uterus.

Still, the original plan of care was put in place to start whenever Omar started his call; when he found out, he immediately told the nurse that he would not carry out this plan of care because this, to him—*would be an abortion.*

The baby was alive, and there was no immediate threat to the mom's health, meaning that there was no evidence that she had an infected uterus and her placenta was not separating off; she was not going into labor on her own.

To Omar, in spite of the chances that she could end up delivering a baby that would either pass away in the womb, pass away shortly after being born or survive but have potentially major disabilities, he didn't believe it was his place to take a life.

"I leave that up to God," my husband expressed to the nursing staff. One of the nurses was crying because while she didn't agree with inducing the patient, she didn't speak up.

After thoroughly talking with the patient about all of her and her baby's risks, Omar offered to transfer her if she wanted to continue the same plan of care or be discharged home with strict warning signs. She ended up deciding to go home. She came back two days later, and another provider induced her. Her baby died at 19 weeks.

My husband was still fighting for life and didn't know what God had called someone to bear. In retrospect, it is the same for us. God does not give up on us just because we're terminally ill, have complications, have disabilities, or are mentally ill. "Before I formed you in the womb I knew you, and before you were born I consecrated you; I appointed you a prophet to the nations" (Jer. 1:5).

Omar told me the night this happened, "God breathed life into us. We are God's design. Thus, every life matters; whether it is an unborn baby or someone battling depression, they are equally valuable to God."

He will fight for your life despite your brokenness. More importantly, he will fight for the life that no one else can see.

Four

Sacrificial Love

*A little too much anger, too often or at the wrong time, can
destroy more than you would ever imagine.*
Marilynne Robinson, *Gilead*

I grabbed the dark green rag and scrubbed the dish; we had
just blown out the candles and put away the leftover
cherry pie in the fridge. He came behind me and brought up
the idea of counseling.

I wanted nothing of it. I didn't want to talk to anyone.
End of story.

"Why would I spend money on someone pretending to
care?" I scrubbed the white plate as hard as I would scour a
dirty tub.

"It's not your money," he shot back, his voice low, as though he instantly regretted it. He started rambling over what he said, but I didn't hear anything.

I grew dizzy and nearly threw the dish down.

"What did you say?" I asked.

He didn't repeat what he said but rambled on about how I needed counseling and how it would heal me.

"That's not what you said!"

I quietly walked away from the kitchen this time, feeling like someone had ripped open all my scar tissues.

"What are you doing?" He turned off the kitchen sink.

"Don't do this again, my love. Come, talk with me."

I ignored him until I had to spew it out. It spilled like the kitchen sink I had left running, my eyes hard and cold.

"I'm drinking because I'm so miserable with you. I knew this entire time that's how you thought of me. I'm just wasting *your* money, right? This is all yours, right? What am I even doing here, then? I don't know why I married you! You don't help me; you *never* help me. You just pray and would rather be in your prayer closet than with me. I'm just here being a nuisance, wasting all your big fat money, right? I hate you," I cried as I ran to our bedroom and slammed the door.

I rummaged through our closet for my bag. He came in.

"I hate you! I'm leaving you because that's what you want, and I'm a waste of *your money*. Congratulations, Omar. That was my last straw," I shouted.

Everything seemed like a hum except the rattling of my voice.

"That's not true, Samantha," he said, "Don't believe that."

"It's true, and I'm sick of living in hell like this. I'd rather be dead than live with you," I walked out of the room and swiftly grabbed a knife without him looking. I slammed the front door. I knew he probably remained in the room, crouched on the floor with his hand over his face.

I drove to a different parking lot on the other side of the complex. I wailed wildly in the cold; it was winter, and everything in this broken moment felt so cold. *I was a waste of money. I was nothing. That's how he saw it, and that's how he would always see it. I could never forgive him for saying it.*

I angrily shouted, "I can't bear this anymore, Father. I can't breathe. I can't do it." I slipped the knife out of my bag, its gleaning edge ready to free me from the pain.

"Good riddance..." I muttered as I traced the knife over my wrist that waited to be cut like a dead mackerel. I pressed in. I wanted him to regret it. I wanted to show him just how much this hurt me.

Beloved.

My eyes shut tight.

Beloved.

I grimaced before I hit the steering wheel, dropped the knife, and wept. My mind raced with evil thoughts, which all crossed the finish line.

I'm a waste of life. No one cares for me. I am no one for anyone to love enough.

Beloved.

I looked to the night sky, the stars barely there. I studied the space above me; *I love you, beloved.*

It felt like this still, small voice tore up the road the lies of the enemy ran on. It was all in my head. I placed the knife in my brown bag and drove home. I opened the door and expected to find Omar on the couch. But instead, I walked over to our bedroom and found him crouched in a ball on the floor of our small dim-lit closet.

"What are you doing?" I asked him, turning to place my bag on the bed. He got up, tears smeared on his wet cheeks, and he looked at me with his brown-reddish eyes. As much at that moment I wished this fight could be over, the anger, the sadness I saw in his eyes, it wasn't. It wasn't over.

"You hurt me," I whispered.

"I know, my love, and I'm sorry I said that. I regretted it the instant it came out of my mouth. I was acting in anger, and I should have never said that to you, my love. I'm sorry," he said, his voice raw.

"It's not enough. I only came back to let you know I'll be leaving tomorrow to my sister's place," I said.

"My love, don't leave. I love you," he said. *No, he doesn't*, the dark voice of the enemy taunted into my ears.

"No, you don't. You love the *idea* of me." *Yes, yes, that's it.*

"Samantha, forgive me. I'm asking you to forgive me..." his eyes looked longing. *Forgive him? He said it's his money in this marriage. He's a liar.* I felt my long, black hair push to the side, so the whispers of the devil grew louder. My eyes filled with tears.

"No. I'll never forgive you. You hate me. You think I'm a

waste of money! I hate you!" I stormed to the other bathroom in our apartment.

I sobbed, slammed the door, and dropped to my knees. Omar came in and picked me up.

"My love," he pushed my knotted black hair from my face.

"I acted in anger and frustration. You are my love, my wife, and I love you more now than I ever have."

"NO!" I yelled, "You don't love me anymore. I'm—"

I gathered my bag when suddenly something crashed in the shower tub. We didn't move for a couple of seconds while looking at each other. My husband peeled back the curtain. The rack bar somehow fell.

"How did—"

"That was God intervening for us," he said while he gathered me in his arms. I felt like something broke in me, like the way an egg suddenly cracks and oozes out. He walked me back to our room, where I sat on the bed and cried into his belly while he stood before me. In some way or another, God wanted me to stay. He didn't want me to give up.

"God is fighting for us," I said through my tears.

"Yes," Omar whispered into my hair as he held me. It took everything to realize the battle I was raging war against wasn't my husband. It was the devil in my mind. I had allowed room for him to take up space and decorate the house of my mind with lies, lies that felt as real as the hand I held at night.

As we got into bed and turned off the lights, I nudged closer to him, and the closer I got, the closer the reality of keeping the truth from him ate at me. While I took his hand in my own, I couldn't help but retrace my memories: the gulping down hard liquor, the secret smoking, the tears while I brushed my teeth and showered to erase the cigar smell. The truth was, I still quietly battled the secrecy of keeping these habits from Omar.

I remember the day I felt *it* and the day the truth spilled out of me like the liquor my husband would pour down the drain that day.

I was in my studio room working when I started wallowing. I opened the drawer and pulled out the El Guitarron liquor. With shaky hands, I unscrewed the cap and gulped as much as possible. Shortly after, I began to feel woozy. I heard the keys jangle as our front door opened. Sitting on the couch, I couldn't have been more wrapped in shame.

"What's wrong, my love? I can see it on your face," he said, walking toward me. Guilt took my hand, and I shook my head in denial.

"I feel so awful...I can't tell you," I whispered, not meeting his eyes.

"My love, did you drink?" he asked, his voice worried yet saddened at the same time. I shook my head.

"Where is it?" he probed gently. "I'm not upset. How much did you drink?" I finally looked at him; his face was full of concern.

"I—a lot," and then I started weeping. I rose and ran to my studio room and fell on the floor in a daze. He came over to me.

"The drawer," I sobbed. I heard the drawer roll open, and

my heart lurched. I saw the blanket fall to the floor. His wedding ring clanked against the jar. Gold reflected on the carpet as the sun hit the bottle. I buried my face in the quilt on the floor. I don't think I've ever felt so small.

Then he bent down. He rocked me back and forth, kissing my head.

"Is this all of it, my love?"

Of course, I assured him that it was.

"How long have you been doing this?"

"I don't know, a couple of months." His eyebrows furrowed, and his lips pursed. "Why do you drink, my love? Why do you do this to yourself?" I didn't answer, but my heart trauma took a hundred steps back.

The memory of someone charging at me and choke-holding me against the wall.

The memory where I'm on the floor, and someone barges in and yells that I'm nothing and screams obscenities at me.

The memory of someone punching someone in front of me, each blow feeling like a ram pummeling my heart with its horns.

The memory of someone screaming like they were being murdered in the other room after verbally abusing me.

The memory of someone saying they're going to kill themselves in a bathtub because of me.

Maybe it was an alloy of all of this and more. My doctor-husband knew my past. He knew my traumas, the couple dozen men I dated, and the despair I put myself in.

Omar could see the horrible pain in my eyes; he took my

shoulder and prayed for me. He stood; moments later, I heard the disposal gulp all that liquor down. I went to the living room and sat down on the couch. He joined me and startled me with a question.

"How would you feel about starting medication?"

"I don't know," I mumbled, the alcohol making me want to lie down.

"I think it would help," he stroked my face. "For the longest time, I think I wanted to deny any sign that you had depression. I wanted to see if I could just fix it with prayer and time, but now that you've turned to substance abuse, I don't think I can ignore it anymore. I don't want the enemy to kill you this way, my love."

Kill me?

I think I was far from that.

My husband was patient for God to change me through his prayers. He sought the Lord for me when I could not pray for myself. Sometimes, I wonder how many grieving husbands wish they could change their wives when they haven't even gotten on their knees to pray for them. My husband intervened for me in a way no one has in my entire life, selflessly.

I'm reminded of the difference it makes when one responds to wrath in love: "A gentle answer turns away wrath, but a harsh word stirs up anger" (Prov. 15:1).

Several weeks after another fight, I found my husband in the parking lot at the back of the apartments. I opened the car door and sat in.

"I think you have borderline personality disorder," he said evenly. His face was firm and his eyes cold.

I chuckled at him and sighed. He looked at me and began reading all the symptoms.

Volatile episodes of anger.

Breaking near objects.

Feelings of emptiness.

Self-harm.

I watched my fingers tighten. I remembered sitting on our chair when I had begun to tear through my skin like sanding through a fish. I balled my body up on the chair and rocked myself to tears.

I was reminded of a poem that spoke grace over my scars. It reminded me that while I feel alone, Christ is preparing bread and wine for me.

O Holy One,
and asked to be fed.
But there is no bread,
no wine,
no priest.
Is there no one to
minister
to me?
Is there no place
at the table for damaged hearts
and scarred souls?...
In spite of an empty table, I believe.

In spite of evidence to the contrary
that they scream in my face,
I will stand at your empty table,
and wait until you come,
your arms full of bread,
the wine splashing as you walk.
Come, O Holy One,
and feed me.[4]

So, I will wait, too. I will yield from the harvest of Christ because this is the bread that nourishes my soul. This is the bread of life, the bread of my Father's life. The healing bread that covers my scars. My husband read on.

Frequent periods of depression. Substance abuse.

I looked at him, steadying my voice before answering slowly, "There's a diagnosis for everything. I don't have a disorder," I said. Regardless of what I uttered, he knew I needed help, and honestly, I knew it too.

A week later, I told him I had cut my wrist. He grabbed the wrong one, then the other, and the profound utterance of grief that spilled from his lips saddened me.

"Why, why, why did you do this to yourself, my love?" And all I could say from my throbbing chest was, "I don't know. I'm stupid. I'm weak."

"We'll get through this together. You're not alone, my love." He squeezed my hand. I pressed it back.

About two weeks later, we went to a psychiatrist for the first time. It was challenging but needed. The psychiatrist ended up diagnosing me with major depressive disorder and traits of borderline personality disorder. He prescribed an antipsychotic medication to take with my anti-depressant. Things slowly changed after a week and a half.

I prayed more, tried to read more, and devoted more time to my Father. I even began to join my husband in the prayer closet, where he would smile and wrap his strong arms around me. We would worship and sing together. We cried together at God's goodness, faithfulness, and redeeming love.

"Omar, do you think I'll always be like this?" I asked.

"I don't know, but I'm here for you. We'll get through this together. I love you."

Is it possible, Jesus, for me to give you glory through my story even amidst still being broken?

I wondered how broken people do this. What does it mean to give glory to Jesus through our brokenness or state of brokenness? For me, it was simple; it looks like raised hands to the Father who has set me free from all of my pain. It looks like setting the dinner table for my husband and me even when I've been battling in my mind. It looks like saying a prayer over someone even when I feel lost that day. It looks like being present for someone else even when I'm battling feeling detached.

Medicine is not what healed me, but it allowed me to breathe and gave me a break from constantly wallowing in my emotions. It allowed me to clear my head and focus more on the additional help I needed for healing. The medication also allowed me to be more open about my problems with a counselor and my close friends. I am choosing to change for the betterment of our marriage, and I have seen the fruit because of it. It took a while to realize the frailty of marriage and how ours was falling between our fingers because of my unwillingness to seek help. I always declined to see a doctor, counselor, or anyone for my mental illness.

We can't see the benefits if we never reach out. I could stay a lifetime in the same place, but I never wanted to be this way; I didn't want to be that stubborn person for my husband or our future children. I remember when we married how explosive I was to him in public, not caring who saw us, not caring how it made him appear. I remember leaving him several times in anger, slapping my fork down, or scooting my plate up before dashing away. Even during our honeymoon, I couldn't withhold my frustrations; we had several arguments in our suite in Santorini, Greece, and all I wanted to do was run away. This was still wrong of me; our marriage could not be built on running away but by drawing closer to Christ.

Even when the steepled church caused that steep hill in my heart, I still needed to push through my episodes to live sacrificially for my husband and to love him well. I had an unholy grudge against the church after living in California for a year and a half; another story for a different time, that season of my life, left me spiritually burned.

I needed a lot of soul work to get to where my husband and I are now. Our marriage was created to glorify God, but I knew there was more behind the *veil* than always having the excuse that I'm a work in progress. I wanted to change through God's grace because I know his grace can change people.

By November 2021, I began seeing a counselor and a spiritual mentor weekly. While some days I can hardly get myself out of bed, I still willingly go because I know it is good for my heart. With my medication, it's often hard to *feel* things, but I'm getting better at choosing to relish in the moments to pursue Jesus with everything in me. I need to be *present* in the small, to be *present* in the large. While I still struggle with my emotions, I realize more and more that I'm less concerned with *feeling present* rather than simply *being still and knowing*. If I am still in the Lord and understand who God is and who he has called me to be, it makes me rest in the *unfeeling*.

Almost a year into our first home, I walked on wooden floors where the sunlight danced, feeling Jesus so near and tangible. Omar was cooking in the kitchen, stirring the meat in the pot. I just stared at him from behind, admiring his simple stature while cooking. My eyes traced his head of black hair, his soft hairy arms, and his gentle hands.

"I love you, Omar. I'm sorry for all the ways I've ever hurt you," I told him with tears. It was so unexpected; he turned toward me and asked why I said that.

"I just want to honor Jesus in our marriage, and I can't do that by hurting you," I said. He put the wooden stirrer on the spoon rest and kissed me then, and I felt the warmth of his love wrap around me.

I would embrace the new heart God would give me: "I will give you a new heart and put a new spirit in you; I will remove

from you your heart of stone and give you a heart of flesh"
(Ezek. 36:26). I would embrace the new person I would become
and do everything in my power to become this person for the
Lord, my husband, our marriage, and *our future children.*

This is what it means to partake of the good harvest before
me. It is nothing I have done but everything Christ has done
for me. I know I will fail if I only tend to my inept garden
and think this is all I have left to give; an entire harvest awaits
us that Jesus broke for and that bread is for us, to grace our
tables and hearts.

Five

Our Sacred Marriage

He has sent me to bind up the brokenhearted...
Isaiah 61:1

It took a while to realize my husband was not made to gratify or satisfy me. My one holy purpose in marriage is glorifying God and pleasing God. Only then can that sacred goodness spill into my marriage like a river. Isn't this the sanctification process of marriage, that by being imitators of Christ and delighting in him, our marriages reflect him? It was as though Jesus's transfiguration became so evident and real that it fostered the transformation in me. It allowed a wild outpouring of grace to heal my marriage. Thus, submitting to one another involves the process of sanctification. It involves honest, hard work.

Later that same day, after telling him I had cut myself, we held onto each other and wept. We caressed and prayed to God that he would begin to change me. It took all of me to do the easiest thing in the world, to surrender and fall into the arms of Christ.

And so, I took it upon myself to surrender daily; I'd awake and pray in the mornings. I knew I needed to sustain my soul in Christ and anchor myself in his Word.

I began to believe evermore that God *will, as long as I am willing,* change me into the likeness of Christ and become the wife I was called to be. And yes, it may be broken and painful at times, but I knew I wanted to stop hurting my husband.

Instead, I wanted to be a fruitful, patient, and ever-loving wife. And thus, the purging slowly began to bear fruit in our marriage. This liturgy, *A Liturgy for Husband & Wife at Close of Day*, from *Every Moment Holy*, speaks to this most.

Husband: I am not strong enough in my own strength to be husband to you.

Wife: And I am not strong enough in my own strength to be wife to you.

Together: Let us turn to God together then, asking the strength that we need...Give us, therefore, the strength that comes from the grace that flows from your heart alone, O God, that we might live and move and breathe in air of that grace, receiving it in ourselves and then offering it daily to one another. Without grace, our marriage will wither as a vine unrooted. But sustained by your grace, it will ever flourish and bloom and flower and fruit.[5]

This liturgy is incredibly applicable to all marriages. When I first read this liturgy, I cried; it felt like this was the groaning of my heart in many ways. I ended up printing it and framing it right outside our bedroom door. That way, it's a constant reminder that apart from God's good grace, we have nothing good to give each other; we will not flower and fruit.

Living out in the country was a good move for us after five years in a bigger city; I don't like the precipitancy of large cities. Being able to look upon the meadows leaves me a bit more stilled, a sort of cessation that leaves me better than I was before. Calmer.

I can leave the rebukers and accusers in my mind and focus on the simple, fragile, graceful things, like the way the milkweeds and cornflowers billow in the wind, or the way the beryl swallows fly together in unison, or the bend and grazing of the cows scattered on the open land.

This is *home* for us; my broken mind enjoys this kind of pastoral serenity, maybe because it leaves room for my thoughts to lope like the steeds do, in a kind of insouciant way. My broken spirit *needs* to see the open spaces: the wildflowers, the pruned orchards, the resting marigolds, and the tenders of the soil. It's good for my battered mind. Sometimes, I feel like my spirit has been so frayed through trauma and pain that it feels unmendable, absent, but then I hear a sweet voice, "The sacrifices of God are a broken spirit, a broken and a contrite heart—these, O God, You will not despise" (Ps. 51:17). That voice is almost like a murmur of the meadows; I hear and feel it when I look out on the pastureland where the horses huddle under the shaded oak trees, and I know it's my Father.

While we are languishing in our brokenness, God still anguishes with us because He meets us in our broken-heartedness and comes close to our agony. It is who he is every day, and nothing can change him.

Every day, I want to die to myself to live given to my husband as the liturgy entails. I desire to be the wife who uses her brokenness for good.

So as long as I strive to die to myself daily, I am faithful to God's calling. Even amidst having a mental illness.

"Once we have opened ourselves to grace, then Christ Himself takes up His dwelling in us. If we suffer, He suffers. We *are* His body here on earth... Isn't this reason enough to make our sufferings a sacrifice of praise?"[6]

Yes, Elisabeth Elliot, *yes*. This truth was from a woman who knew pain and suffering well, who lost her husband to the people she would minister to for two years afterward. I can't imagine losing my one and only husband; it's one of my fears. I often whisper my fear to Omar while we lay in bed. He gathered my face in his soft hands and smiled, "Just love me well here. Only God knows when I'm going home." I smile back and say, "Yes, you're right. He knows when we're going home together." We chuckle like two kids.

Nearly half a year after I had hurt myself, I remember preparing fresh soil for our garden beds. We wanted to plant blackberries, strawberries, peppers, zucchini, carrots, and to-matoes. As I'm out in the backyard working with the soil and the seeds, my hands smelling like earth, I can't help but won-der, is this God-glorifying? These ordinary things, like playing with dirt, folding laundry, washing dishes, and cooking meals, are they a part of the grander story? While I'm hand-deep in the dirt, is this what the God story looks like? Does our marriage reflect this?

Omar comes home tired from tending to patients and being hand-deep in surgeries, and he kisses me gently on the lips. *How are you, my love?* He never fails to ask, even now. His clogs have blood stains, and my hands have dirt stains, but we still come together daily. Then he scoops me up, and my wife-heart bursts with joy; after dinner, he washes the dishes and puts them away. He tells me to relax on the couch, but all I want to do is be together, forgetting the dishes or the laundry or the loads.

Surely, this is something of the foundation to which Christ calls a godly marriage; through the tiredness and sacrifice of time, we still serve each other well. We team together to make life easier for one another.

I'm reminded ever so surely, yes, what I am doing is honor-ing God because it is also in the mundane moments that can glorify God. The love I offer to my husband can come from this grace pouring out of myself. I'm reminded of Elisabeth Elliot's book that reads:

Ordinary things can be very holy and very full of God. They are not "religious" things, they are plain, earthly things. We may hope for visions and revelations and 'wonderful experiences,' forgetting that the context of the revelation of God to each of His children is *exactly where that one is*, here, on earth, in this house, this kitchen, this stove, in this family, or at this desk, in this schoolroom, on this tractor or assembly line, this perhaps (to us) very unsatisfactory arrangement of things.[6]

You are serving God by serving your spouse well and whatever else he called you to. Christ came to serve, so we are here to serve; *pour us out, Lord, as a pitcher of water ready to nourish those around us.* I remember feeling like a wanderer, always thinking I was never doing enough for the Kingdom because I wasn't living in a third-world country. I felt inferior because I wasn't a *real missionary*.

"But you are the most mission-hearted person I know, Samantha," a dear friend once told me over tea. I'll never forget her words because it wasn't until later that they truly resonated with me. It took me years to realize that God is not more for me because my hands are toiling in a third-world country versus working in the walls of my home or a classroom. I had always felt like I was not offering much of anything. *What am I putting on the table?*

When I was a little girl, red sketchbooks would be filled page to page; I'd sketch kittens, jars, many stars, and dream houses. My art grew with me; I minored in studio art and won a Best-of-Show award at an annual art show. Sometimes, I think how if I had given my all to painting, I'd probably be a successful artist by now, but it just didn't pan out that way.

Within a year of our marriage, I had completed my Master of Fine Arts in Writing and landed a wonderful teaching job for two years. Omar gently tried to sway me into staying home with our future children, but I resisted. I would remain to teach, and our children would go to daycare, period. I was so adamant that I remained to teach that my mind shut off the idea of ever staying home because why if after all my hard work of getting the degrees, interning, and publishing, would I throw it all away to stay home? What would other people think of me? Some people didn't shy away from what they thought. One time, my husband and I went to see houses with our real estate agent, and the owners were *all about my husband,* never once looking at me. Our agent had to gesture toward me and mention that I was a teacher. They barely looked at me. My heart couldn't wait to get outside and get home; Omar realized what had happened without me saying anything.

At a different time, as I was about to sit with friends for dinner, the guy said, "Michael Kors?" gesturing towards my bag. Surprised, I just laughed it off and said, "Nope. Target. $20." I couldn't stop ruminating on that statement, though. How many people think I'm a Michael Kors-caring type of person? I'm not going to sit here and woe you with statements that hurt my feelings, but comments like this hurt me.

Being a physician's wife does not solve your woes the same way a million bucks can't cure cancer. I'd whisper to my husband at night with tears in my eyes, "You know I could give a rat's butt about name brands, right? Like seriously, it all disgusts me," I wiped my tears.

"I know, my love. I love you, your simple heart, and how the simple things bring you joy." He smiled. My heart pieced itself to sleep with those words.

As I neared the end of the school year and said goodbye to my students, my six-month pregnant body ached to tell my husband something: I was staying home with our children.

He held me and stroked my hair with tears in his brown eyes. "There's no one else more perfect for raising our babies, my love. I'm so proud of you."

I wept long in his arms, not because I was going to miss my career or feel I'd never measure up to people, but because I finally had peace, *a peace just for me*. Elisabeth Elliot said it perfectly about this season of my life over a painting of a rose by Lilias Trotter:

A woman of her generation could not imagine giving up her job, her prestige, and her freedom in order to be a mother. That was too high a price to pay. But as she grew in grace, she saw that giving herself to God meant giving Him everything—death to herself. Then He showed her that motherhood was His call, and when she obeyed, she found not only peace but joys she had not dreamed of. Her yielding (a 'death') meant that a richer life had begun to work in her heart, and wistful thoughts of all she had left behind (the 'petals' that the calyx has let go) were forgotten in her happy embracing of that life.[6]

Trust me when I say this road was hard to accept, but it was something God called me to. He called me to bear fruit in our marriage and through motherhood.

I am the true vine, and my Father is the gardener. He cuts off every branch in me that bears no fruit, while every branch that does bear fruit he prunes so that it will be even more fruitful. You are already clean because of the word I have spoken to you. Remain in me, as I also remain in you. No branch can bear fruit by itself; it must remain in the vine. Neither can you bear fruit unless you remain in me.

I am the vine; you are the branches. If you remain in me and I in you, you will bear much fruit; apart from me you can do nothing. If you do not remain in me, you are like a branch that is thrown away and withers; such branches are picked up, thrown into the fire and burned. If you remain in me and my words remain in you, ask whatever you wish, and it will be done for you. This is to my Father's glory, that you bear much fruit, showing yourselves to be my disciples. (John 15:1-8)

Cultivating the soil is hard work; one must prepare it well to yield a healthy harvest. Most fruit trees take several years to produce ripe fruit, hence why so many of us enjoy grafted trees we can just purchase and plant in our backyard. We don't need to wait seven or ten years for the fruit to flower. The remarkable thing, though, is this: Jesus already did the hard and holy work for us on the cross (John 17:4). The foundation lay in the two beams on which Christ was hung. It is our job to *abide* by this foundation to bear fruit; he's given us the *grafted trees through grace*. It is our job to tend to it and produce even more fruit. It takes abiding, though. According to Merriam-Webster, the word *abide* comes in a transitive and intransitive verb form, meaning several definitions such as: to bear patiently, to endure without yielding, to wait for, to accept without objection, to remain stable or fixed in a state, and, to continue in a place. I once thought abiding in Christ meant simply hiding under his wing, untouched from the rest of the world, as though abiding meant *hiding*. On the contrary, I now realize it's much more about remaining present in Christ and fixed completely on him through the despairs and woes of life because it's during these frail happenstances that the testing of our faith comes. I need to abide in his Word. I need to abide in who he says he is: comforter (Isa. 51:12), sacred shelter (Ps. 27:5), and intercessor on my behalf (Heb. 7:25).

I'd cling to these truths during my greatest despondencies because without them, I believe many of us know too well how close death can seem. But the hope is so tangible now, it's so near. So, yes, Jesus did the hard and holy work on the cross to pay for the penalty of our sins, but we must remember that he simply never stops interceding on our behalf. The moment this truth struck me, tears welled in my eyes because I imagined Jesus interceding for my sins; while I've drank, smoked, and verbally abused my husband, Christ is holding my battered heart up before the Father, pleading on my behalf.

This isn't her. This is her heart. She's a hurting lamb, Father.

Do the hard and good work of reading his Word and abiding in them. In this way, we can commune with him and love him evermore for the sacrifice he has made for us. In this way, we can begin to accept the call he has put upon our lives with joy. In this way, we can pick up our cross with uttermost pleasure. In this way, we can dig deep into the soils of life, tend to what needs tending, and believe in the coming harvest. And when we don't see that choice fruit, we never forget that this is why Christ has given us *grafted trees through grace.*

My roots are inside the home now; it is hard work and sacred work. So much of me was wrapped up in the pursuit of my career. I was going to be a journalist and work for a newspaper, a job I turned down on the Gulf of Texas. I was going to dedicate my mind to the craft of writing editorials and hard news. I was going to use my voice to speak up for others, tell their stories, and tell the truth. In some way, I am still doing this; I share others' stories and the matters of their hearts through a Christian literary platform called *Calla Press*, a journal I established in 2017. Through creative writing, I share the truth of the gospel, and it is my joy.

While God prepared my husband and me for the coming of our children, I know it was more than just *equipping* us; it was as though he was carving our hearts in such a way as to make room. Still, post-partum depression raised her cry out the moment my son took his first breath of cold air.

Part Two

BATTLING MENTAL ILLNESS IN MOTHERHOOD

Six

Post-Partum Depression

The humblest tasks get beautified if loving hands do them.
Louisa May Alcott, *Little Women*

I walked into the hospital's labor and delivery floor, my belly still egg-shaped and soft from being full of our son that was just delivered that week, and I heard a woman wailing in agony and distress. I look at the nurses behind their computer screens, and they give me that sanctioning look.

"Dr. Cabrera's patient," one of the nurses smiled at me. "She didn't want an epidural," she added, brows raised.

I looked at my wide-eyed son sitting on the tech's lap, cooing as newborns do, and I couldn't help but relate to that woman's wailing, except my wailing came after my son was born and in the very walls of what is supposed to be our sacred home, of what is supposed to be my *sacred burden*.

My husband rounded the corner after scrubbing off and saw us waiting; he smiled, kissed our son's yellowish cheek, and took my hand. *Home?* He would ask, and we'd smile *yes* together.

He would take my hand a thousand times, always gently, ready to bring me *back home. Home* from my wayfaring mind when it should have been *willing. Home* from my mercenary ways when they should have been *merciful. Home* from my manic episodes that would leave me wailing like the mother I heard on the third delivery floor.

Our son was born on August 17, 2020, at 9:55 a.m. Seeing that I was stable and wanted to get pregnant, my psychiatrist weaned me off my medications. While my husband warned me about PPD, I told him I'd manage.

Little did I know that it would feel like I had taken one thousand steps backward and become *the burden* I once was before. "After giving birth, approximately 15% of women will experience postpartum depression...." [7]

I was one of them.

I'd cradle my son close so he can feel the fullness of my love, even when my body is breaking and my heart cracks under familial heartache. So he can know what sacrificial love feels like, I live open and give to my son even when my chest feels tight and my lungs can hardly breathe.

Mental illness is as debilitating as it is onerous; one day, I'm cleaning up spilled milk while my son bathes in tomato soup he just tipped over, and I wonder how a mother can do it all. How can a mama live broken open while trying not to break apart?

As my son grew, I'd watch him crawl like a sand crab as I chased after him, my hips burning and my head throbbing, knowing I needed to push through my languid longing for a nap.

I thought when I bore my son, my brokenness would be dormant, and I could function as a mother and maintain some notion of normalcy. Unfortunately, mental illness doesn't disappear when your body tears open to give life passed in a bundle in your arms.

It doesn't disappear because you're supposed to be this new, joyous mother.

Your brain's functions change during motherhood.[7] There's a lot of science behind this, but know this, your brain changes when you become a mother.

I didn't know what to expect when my son was born; I would accept the unfamiliar, but I didn't know postpartum depression was so enfeebling. Everything got to me: my changed body, the stress of breastfeeding, the pressure of pumping, the colic cries from my son, the sleeplessness, and the dishes always in the sink. I couldn't do it all.

My husband would look at me under the pewter moonlight while our two-week-old son slept in his bassinet beside our bed and ask how I was, wanting my heart to be *open and vulnerable.*

I would bemoan the question, knowing I had to wake in two hours to nurse while I felt separated from *all that was me*. I would say OK and turn over while tears seeped into my white pillow, and my husband would turn me over again and whisper consoling Christ-exalting truths into my hair: "You're an amazing mom. I'm so proud of you, mama."

"How can I feel so torn apart when we have the most beautiful son sleeping beside me?" I asked. My husband would caress my face and tell me how we'll get through this PPD together, and that was not alone, however long it would take.

I lost 30 pounds in his first two weeks of life. Food didn't nourish my body while anxiety filled me and depression sat in my dark eyes. Red rashes grew upon my legs, PUPPS on my flabby belly, and I was bleeding from my second-degree tear, where an allergic reaction sprouted from the pads I wore. I was miserable, and hell felt so close. I hated showering to feel the dreadful sting of the shower head. My doctor-husband would sweep in to take care of me, grab me medicine, and shower me with sacrificial love in the middle of the night while the pain felt like a rash inside me that I could not itch. I remember leaning over to him while our baby still slept, and I whispered how I wanted to *hurt my body in some broken, messed-up way*. He shot up in bed like a rocket and asked me what I wanted to do to myself, and I didn't have an answer except to tell him quietly that I needed to start up again on medicine.

During our son's third week, I started back up on my SSRI. That's the thing with recurrent major depressive disorder; it comes again.

I can hardly write this without breaking into tears because I *know* that while I felt alone in my suffering, I wasn't. Other mamas were suffering right there beside me, on the same night, all across the world. There were and still are so many mamas breaking under the weight of it all, and my heart stretches wide open, making room for them, for you. I want to take your hand so badly and tell you: *don't give in because his harvest is enough for us all.*

PPD is real. It's as real as the babe you hold in your arms. You hear the tragedies, the mamas who can't bear it, the mamas or papas who take their lives. My heart breaks for them. My heart breaks for *you*. You may be alone in your household with your babe, doing all the house tending, like the dishes and the laundry, but you are never alone.

There are more than 11 million other moms and dads at home in this country doing the same thing you are. More importantly, it needs to say, Jesus is tending the dishes with you. He's folding that old tattered red shirt your husband loves to wear. He's smiling while you gaze at your wee one playing with a train set. And he's weeping with you, too. He holds you while you cry on the toilet seat, wondering if it gets better. He embraces you when you pause at the kitchen sink, heaving, silently weeping because you feel you'll never get this mother thing right and that you've lost who you are.

Jesus, be with her, with you. Be with the woman who wails. Be with the woman who weeps. Be with the man who breaks under pressure. Be with the man who can't grapple with his wife's emotions. Be with the parents who grieve. Be with the parents who don't understand. Be with those who feel like they are becoming undone.

Motherhood undid every part of me. Maybe it did for you, too. I remember feeding my son while my body felt like it was slowly breaking apart. I can truly say I daily died to myself to live entirely given to my son; I was going through the worst of my relapsing depression.

Perhaps God sacrificed his son so I would know, amidst my brokenness, how to love my son sacrificially. And in this feat, I would welcome my brokenness because it willed me to *be present* for my son, to change his soiled diapers, to read stories of hungry caterpillars or mischievous rabbits, or to help his tiny fingers grasp his wooden train set.

Being present is difficult for me suffering from bouts of de-realization. I watch my son play with his toy dinosaurs while the beam on my face feels like a thousand miles away. I often find myself looking out the clear windows, thinking how my body is growing wider, rounder, weirder even, and I'm hearing my son blowing raspberries, and I yearn *to feel some normalcy through this.*

But normalcy wouldn't come. I never felt fully alive. Never quite real.

When my husband and I took a short mission trip to Uganda, I painted murals on caked-mud walls, laughed with orphan children, and prayed with the mothers. I'll never forget seeing the wading crocodiles and hippopotamuses in the Nile, nor the smiles of the women while they cooked, or hung their mussed dresses on the clothesline. The funny thing is when I think back on this time, I instantly think of the simple nature of things: how the young boys would make a toy car out of a can of Coca-Cola, wheels made from paper clips, and they'd pull it along with string, or the joy the children would get holding the squeaking soft-yellow chicks, or how a four-year-old was already doing his own laundry in a tin bucket.

I remember struggling carting around my suitcase of art supplies when several of the children ran up to me and grabbed all my things to help me carry it to the house. When they saw I was going to their house, they started clapping and saying they wanted monkeys on their wall. I giggled with them and said how I was going to paint a galaxy of stars and planets for them. They cheered and asked for me to "draw monkey". So, I painted them a little family of monkeys among the moon amongst the stars. My heart swelled with adoration and thanksgiving in these moments, because it really does set your life right—enjoying the simple things bring great joy. We celebrate and adore a very vast God who enjoys giving his children the pleasures of their hearts, even if it's as simple as monkeys on a moon.

It was a time I'll never forget. My husband performed OB services while we were there. I remember I wanted to visit him after making lunch with the children. I started walking in the hospital's general direction when a young African man pulled beside me to offer me a ride on his motorcycle. It did save me twenty minutes walking in the heat.

When I walked in, I found Omar tending to a patient. He was working alongside another doctor who served there as a missionary.

Suddenly, I heard the cry. It was a wailing. I listened to the weeping. I looked at the woman lamenting and saw that she had lost her baby to Malaria.

The pain on her face is something I'll never forget. She looked torn apart as she bent forward and backward, writhing in pain and loss. She was wailing, "Oh, God. Oh, God."

How can just a couple of miles down the dirt road be praises sung loudly, and then there's here, the breaking of life, the breaking of hearts? I didn't understand why such an innocent life was taken away.

I remember going into a different room where a premature was just delivered. He needed incubation. I remember studying this tiny life, barely making it on the table; his dark skin was so innocent and so frail and I just thought: *why, God?*

Why is there so much suffering for the innocent? Why does there have to be *any* suffering for the innocent? And then I remember how God uses pain to heal and uses suffering to strengthen—*sufferers*—for his holy story. I'm softly reminded of John 3:16: "For God so loved the world that he gave his one and only Son, that whoever believes in him shall not perish but have eternal life." In his radical love for us, he died for us; his anguish gave us *eternal hope*.

So often, amidst battling mental illness, we can forget this. The startling truth is that *God died for you*; he didn't die so we could sing hymns and songs on Sunday morning, read a few Christian books on a summer day, and maybe utter a bedtime prayer from tired lips.

God stooped low in love to reach for that sin in your hands, took it upon his back, and carried it up to Calvary, so *you* don't have to die to it. That is love. That is a love you will not find anywhere else.

He loves you.

He didn't die and suffer for *the you* at work, shuffling yellow sticky notes and counting down the hours, or *the you* at church even, putting a smile on for everyone in the holy place.

He died for *the you* at home while your chicken thighs burns in the oven because you were too busy yelling at your family, for *the you* in the closet alone weeping with heaps of baby clothes around you, for *the you* in your bedroom considering if your life is meaningless. He cares for you more than you will *ever* know.

Consider the ravens: They do not sow or reap, they have no storeroom or barn; yet God feeds them. And how much more valuable you are than birds! Who of you by worrying can add a single hour to your life? Since you cannot do this very little thing, why do you worry about the rest?

Consider how the wild flowers grow. They do not labor or spin. Yet I tell you, not even Solomon in all his splendor was dressed like one of these. 28 If that is how God clothes the grass of the field, which is here today, and tomorrow is thrown into the fire, how much more will he clothe you—you of little faith! (Luke 12:24-28)

God suffered so we can trust him with our own sufferings. It's because he suffered that he is able to *empathize* with us. He suffered so we can *rejoice in our sufferings.*

"More than that, we rejoice in our sufferings, knowing that suffering produces endurance, and endurance produces character, and character produces hope, and hope does not put us to shame, because God's love has been poured into our hearts through the Holy Spirit who has been given to us." (Rom. 5:3-5)

The Lord uses suffering to accomplish his purposes. It is so, friend; the Lord uses *your* suffering for his purposes in *you*. Your calvary of the mind is not too grievous for Emmanuel to cover. Depression is a real kind of suffering. David experienced it while he wrote psalms of lament. You can hear his cry, his despair, his brokenness.

> "Depression is a disease (i.e., it is the absence of health), an illness (i.e., it has consequences known only to the sufferer), and a sickness (i.e., there are social consequences). When we see depression through these lenses, we can appreciate how comprehensive and convoluted it is."[8]

Depression is a sickness like any sickness that ails an organ. It's been traced back to biblical times; these people aren't just biblical characters of a giant make-believe story; they were real people like you and me. David wrote out his depression in ways millions of people can relate to. While you hear his weeping, you can hear his *worship*, too. Psalms were meant to be sung as a means of worship to God; is it then possible to sing sorrow? Can it be an act of worship to God to give thanks even through anguish? David would say so. He wrote some of the psalms while hiding in the desert or caves; in fact, he wrote Psalm 142 in a cave alone. This was David's lament and his prayer.

> I cry aloud to the Lord;
>> I lift up my voice to the Lord for mercy.
> I pour out before him my complaint;
>> before him I tell my trouble.
>
> When my spirit grows faint within me,
>> it is you who watch over my way. (Psalm 142:1-3)

Remember, God uses anguish to accomplish his purposes, and now we have these psalms to remind us that God is with us in our woes. Sometimes, God uses lament to bring us out of depravity; it may fill our whole being, but there is something to rejoice about. The Savior is near us in our lament and understands it most (Matt. 27:46). His dying expresses the most profound anguish, and he laments with us because God himself wept *for us*.

> Nothing in all creation is hidden from God's sight. Everything is uncovered and laid bare before the eyes of him to whom we must give account. Therefore, since we have a great high priest who has ascended into heaven, Jesus the Son of God, let us hold firmly to the faith we profess. For we do not have a high priest who is unable to empathize with our weaknesses, but we have one who has been tempted in every way, just as we are—yet he did not sin. (Heb. 4:12-16)

Thus, no depression or disorder is too deep for an anguishing God not to suffer and be with us in. While we feel lost in our mental calvary, that is where God is at home.

Seven

The Surrendering

Your greatest contribution to the kingdom of God might not
be something you do, but someone you raise.
Andy Stanley

Still in bed, I looked at the stretched golden fields through
our bedroom window and cried out how I wanted to live
entirely given to my family amidst my mental state.

I felt my heart open more as I slowly gleaned from the
harvest before me, God's harvest of grace and goodness.

I breathed in and out. Living given is to show up.

I needed to show up even when I felt detached. I needed
to show up even when I felt like breaking down. There is a
harvest if we do not relent (Gal. 6:9).

I pulled off the flower-patterned quilt and went to my son, who was crying. I scooped him up and carried him to the rocker. While I held my almost one-year-old son on my lap with the milk bottle his papa had already prepared and left outside his bedroom door that morning, I whispered a prayer: *Oh, Father, sustain me this day. I surrender my thoughts and my emotions to you. I want to be fully present for my son today. I want to do everything with dignity and desire to be holy before you. Help me be the wife and mother you've called me to be today. Amen.*

My son looked up at me, and I brushed my lips on his tawny hair and kissed him. I felt the joy close in on me, knowing I'd be showing up today as I let my son slide down my legs to crawl to his toys. He gravitates to animals and pop-up books.

Together with the *very* hungry caterpillar, we've devoured a lot of food, colors, and words; it happens to be one of the most joyous moments throughout my day because my mind is focused on living given to my son and not how fractured my thoughts are. I watched his eyes soak in the shapes and sounds, and it was in these moments that peace spilled into my soul. I feel like this is where I'm meant to be, unseen to the rest of the world but entirely seen through my little boy's eyes.

I realized when I am fully surrendered to my family, this is when I truly live in abundance. This is when I live entirely given to the One my soul loves and the ones I've been blessed to love.

However, as the day progressed, I felt my hands start clutching my emotions all over again. The surrendering I had prayed for somehow began to fade. Something unsettled me; I couldn't pinpoint what had happened from the morning until sunset. I tried to ignore it, given that today was a special day.

I walked down the stairs to prepare dinner for my family. It would be our son's special dinner. Our farm table is a long carved wooden piece that can sit ten souls, but I crave the three of us at the dinner table.

My husband walked in and kissed me. His eyes glowed, and everything in me melted to love him more deeply. I tried to put my fickle feelings aside. I served us while Omar kissed Elias and sat him in his chair. I prepared everything for him, including a blueberry muffin and a single blue Crayon candle.

"How was your day, my love?" Omar asked over a bite of sorrel pasta.

"It was good," I say while chopping up spaghetti on Elias's tray table.

"What made it good?" He continues. My past character would be churlish by now, but I told him all the good things that happened that day. I didn't realize he was tenderly gazing at me while I spoke. He grabbed my hand and brushed it with his fingers.

"I'm proud of you, my love. I want every day to be like that for you and our son. Don't give up."

I never had the intention of giving up. Yet, isn't this the misfortune of depression? Some days, I feel like I can do all the housework and motherly things, and on others, I feel paralyzed.

Then, it happens again, and I become the despondent wife and mother I always dreaded being.

We laughed and joked over dinner with our sweet son.

Today was Elias' first birthday.

I was pleasantly surprised by how well our baby ate his chopped-up spaghetti.

"Feliz cumpleaños, mi bebe," I heard my husband's voice murmur as he drew his face close to our son.

I got up and prepared the muffin, and lit the candle. Then, after singing, we blew it out for him and kissed him.

We sat back down to enjoy the evening. I remember making a quick comment about our son that he disregarded.

It all happened so fast.

"No, that's not right," he made some notion that made me feel stupid. I stifled my urge to blow up until I got pressed. All I remember is being sullen and cross after that, giving him short answers.

We didn't expect our evening to turn so quickly. My emotions went from feeling like an idyllic afternoon picnic to a terrorizing tornado in seconds.

"What's wrong?" He asked me. I said I was fine and started rinsing the reddish-stained plates in the sink.

"What is it?" He pressed, and I felt the match strike in my broken soul, and I spewed out the hate that moiled inside me in front of our birthday boy.

"You're just an over-controlling moron who thinks he knows it all. It's annoying," I said as I walked away. Omar's brows furrowed.

"You have no respect for Elias," my husband murmured under an angry breath. "Happy birthday, Elias," he finished.

"Oh, you're so innocent. You're the good parent. I'm the evil one!" I yelled. I heard a soft whimper from our son, and my heart lurched; he was scared.

I picked up Elias and took him breathlessly up the stairs, leaving my husband in the kitchen. Elias was all a bundle of silence as I changed him and finally sat on the light grey rocker. I sighed as I picked up his milk bottle.

I wept into his light brown hair that I could feel tickling my wet left cheek while my body convulsed silently. I ruined the evening.

I brushed his soft cheek with my finger and heard his tiny throat gulp down the milk, slowly drifting into dreamland.

I gathered the strength in my 23-week pregnant body to lift my 24-pound son to his wooden crib. I placed him gently over; he stuck his little butt in the air like he always does.

"Rest well, my little prince. Happy birthday," I whispered as I ran my hand along the crib rail.

As I gently closed the door, I felt the rage churn inside me, knowing I'd still need to confront my husband.

I had a plan to run away.

I hastily walked downstairs and grabbed the keys on the kitchen counter.

"Where are you going? Come back, my love," my husband pleaded at the garage door.

"I'm done here. You have no idea what my day is like taking care of our baby and then having the decency to correct me on something. How would you know? *I'm* the one who knows these things," I shouted.

I was spent and fed up and completely miffed. My eyes grew hot as I jumped into the driver's seat while my husband was standing in front of the car. My thoughts raced. *You know you don't want to do this, so stop, go home. You know you always go home, anyways.*

I slammed my door shut and drove off down our country road. As I passed wildflowers and maple trees, I saw the horses galloping, suddenly remembering how our backdoor neighbors stilled and quieted their horses with soft touches.

Isn't this all too familiar to God? I stormed off only to find myself parked under the shade of an oak tree, where I wept until I heard him. *Go back home, beloved. Come home.*

Everything in me wants to rage and rage until the moonlight settles in to make him suffer my absence, but the God in me moves me and drives me home.

I find him on the couch, hands in his black hair, head down.

"Did I come back home just to look at you sulk?" I spoke.

Omar looked up; his face was pink from crying, long and dejected from sorrow.

"What's wrong, my love? What has you so discontented in life? What just happened?" his voice was raspy. I glared at him for a while, feeling my fury rise.

"It's you! It's you and your control and your self-righteousness!" I yelled as I ran off into our guestroom and slammed the door shut. A wail came out of me, a bemoaning that could have shaken our home apart. As I was about to get up, he came in.

"Go away. I want to be left alone," I said hoarsely.

"And I want to be left together," he smiled and came to me.

"Stop smiling. I'm so angry at you right now," I choked tears.

He cupped my face, tears now seeping into his brown eyes.

"We are one, my love. We're one. Why would I ever want to hurt you?" he cried softly, his eyes growing big to emphasize his words. "If I hurt you, I'm also hurting myself."

It was all too much. He didn't mean it when it came down to the nitty-gritty of life; I threw his hands off. Perhaps in this broken state of mine, I felt rejection, as though he thought I wasn't doing something right.

"No!" I screamed. "You make me feel like I'm not good enough," I yelled.

"My love, please don't do this," he pleaded. I was like a wild stallion caught by a rope wanting desperately to run.

I grabbed the white picture frames hung on the wall of our family and crashed them into the corner of the wall.

This will show him. This will show him not to treat me less than him. My irrational thoughts spun as wildly as a tornado.

He came to me and tried to hold me in his arms.

"Leave me alone. Let me go!" I yelled like a mad woman as he tried to hold me down. We fell onto the bed. "I hate you. I hate you!"

He cried out, "God! Please save my wife! Please help her. Please help my wife!"

In his voice was a cry I had never heard before, full of suffering and pleading. I can still hear that cry to this day.

I looked at his red-brimmed, puffy eyes and grew quiet. We lay beside one another on the bed.

He ran his hands through my hair quietly, and I felt his soft lips kiss my temple. "You're my other half. I love you so much," he cried into my hair.

"I love you, Omar. I'm sorry. I don't know what came over me," I sobbed. He held me tightly.

We breathed in and out like two tired stallions. I just wanted to rest. After picking up the shards of glass and vacuuming, we slowly walked up the stairs together and peeked in on our sleeping one-year-old in his lion-patterned sleep sack.

Omar bent low and kissed our son. Elias lightly stirred.

I breathed in, watching them. This is going to be a journey. The road to healing is never easy, but don't forget to yield from my harvest, beloved.

I could go on and on about how the evening of our son's birthday was ruined and the shame that plagued me, but I will say this: my husband and I are both broken, imperfect people, and we both said broken things to each other.

What broke me even more was when I saw our son's unopened birthday card on our farm table the following day. Two smiling parents had already snuffed out the candles after a chorus of a "Happy Birthday" was sung, but our one-year-old didn't get to hear the sweet voice of his papa reading what he wrote to him in Spanish for his first birthday. I think this broke my heart, and I started tearing up while I fed my son some banana-crème yogurt. "We'll read your birthday card today, my little prince," I grinned at him while his little mouth was covered in yogurt.

While my husband was probably holding up silver forceps, I held my phone up to reveal how painstakingly sorry I was for causing his heart to break last night. I hadn't expected him to see my messages so quickly, and my heart started weeping gratefulness. He called me, and I cried with him. "I love you. We're a team," he said, practically hugging me through the phone.

"I have two tubals today, so I'll get home by 2:30, hopefully. They're back-to-back," he said, and I smiled, thinking how we're back-to-back, too.

After breakfast, I packed Elias up for the park. As we passed wheat fields and cows wading in the pond, I couldn't help but feel jubilation. My son was strapped in the back, playing with a rattly ram toy, and my eyes swelled with tears.

How, God? How do you do it? Even after I've broken your heart from my brokenness, you still lavish me with so much: my husband, our son, our dwelling place, even now, this holy moment. I thank you, Father, for trusting me with this life and the little life you've given me to nurture well.

Living in sacrificial motherhood is like a daily surrendering of my desires; I willingly lay them down at the feet of Christ so I can willfully do the things for my child wholeheartedly.

Does my body ache for a nap or a quiet space to work? Almost every day, but I know these moments are like a passerby on the road home, significant yet fleeting, and I take every moment in. Like when my one-year-old son walked to me like a newborn giraffe and rested his soft head on my rounding belly. He lifted his head back and looked at me, putting his tiny hands on my stomach.

"Pfff," he uttered, with his chocolate eyes melting me.

"What is it, my little prince?" I smiled at him, cupping his face.

"Adah!" He shouted, and I perked up. Apparently, in Hebrew, *Adah* means *beautiful*. Did he know? Did he know of the growing life inside my 23-week round belly? I smiled and bent to kiss his full cheeks.

"Yes, my sweet darling boy, are you ready for your little sister to get here? She's 23 weeks today," I squealed as I picked him up and cuddled him.

"Adah! Pfff," he blubbers, and I laugh while we carry each other out. I, holding his tiny body, and he, holding my battered soul up a bit.

I think of my vacillating heart and how it matters to surrender fully; it's when I surrender that my husband's words come true: "We no longer fight against each other, but we fight for each other."

This is it. This is the only way we should fight, the only fights I desire for our children to see—*through surrendering*.

Eight

❦

Living Given in Motherhood

As one whom his mother comforts, so I will comfort you.
Isaiah 66:13

I woke up to muffled cries at 2:30 a.m. and pulled the waffle-patterned blanket off to tend to my crying son. He felt feverish and hot to the touch. It turned out he was battling a viral infection, and all I could do was bring him close to my colder body and rock him to sleep after filling him with milk. I held his bottle while we swayed back and forth.

Living given looks a lot like this, friends; when we are broken-hearted, tired, and restless, we run to the aching and restless to help them rest. It's sacrificial motherhood. It's sacrificial living. It's giving your life away for serving others so one day they can know what it means to live Christ-like. Isn't this what our crucified Christ did at Calvary?

When my body runs on tepid coffee and simple prayers, living given is picking up my son from his crib to cut strawberries and make him French toast in the early mornings. It's tickling him even when my heart is anguishing so that he can giggle.

It's playing peek-a-boo with him in the backseat while tears run down my face. It's cherishing the repetitiveness of motherhood; or, as some would say, the mundane. We get up every morning to cradle, feed, play, and tend to our babies while the house floors need mopping and the hard-crusted, spaghetti-stained dishes need washing. We don't bother reading until bedtime because we'll hear the clickety-clack of our kid's train set on the floors. We don't bother showering during the day, but we don't groan about these things. Instead, it is an opportunity to whisper thanksgiving to God. While some days my son's temper tantrums distress me, other days I know this house will be the only house that gives him the room to do so. Our wooden floors are the floors his little body wiggles on in frustration, the floors that catch his tears, and all I can do is stoop and hold him.

It is the same with my Father's house and with my Father's table; anyone is welcome, even those like me who throw adult temper tantrums. My God stoops and holds me close. He holds you close, too.

I sometimes stare into the open blue skies, feel the wind calm my face, and think about heaven. After our bodies break, we will face the Savior, and holy repetition will spill from our lips in adoring worship of our Father. It will be exalted. It will be glorious. It will be good.

This is good news for us mothers whose daily lives look a lot like sacrificial living; it is a form of worship in the daily surrendering of ourselves. It happens when our tired lids open, having the urge to go to the bathroom, only to rush straight to our babe's nurseries. This is the daily dying to ourselves to live for another. It's a beautiful exchange. It's motherhood at its core.

But it will never be easy. John 12:24 tells us, "Very truly I tell you, unless a kernel of wheat falls to the ground and dies, it remains only a single seed. But if it dies, it produces many seeds."

Therefore, aren't we created to die to ourselves to live holy? It can be a frightening thought, but hasn't death lost its sting on the cross where Jesus's body was stung for us?

Therefore, we bear fruit in breaking ourselves, like the kernel of wheat. When we lapse and fall amongst the ground, that's when God breaks ground inside us.

We don't need to live afraid of being broken from the daily ongoings of rushed motherhood, mental illness, or even our struggling marriages. What if we turned around in each of these seasons and remembered the closeness of Christ? In the breaking of ourselves, God is breathing new life into us while breaking what needs to be broken. As unusual as it sounds, what if we realized these moments were the actual gifts?

These broken moments are holy, not because we make them out to be, but because a sacred God meets us in the gritty brokenness and does not leave us alone. Instead, he's cultivating new life.

Motherhood was created to live given and wholly to someone every day, putting aside yourself for the sake of someone else. From the beginning, maternity was designed to be a sacrificial way of life. Mary knew she would have to give up her son for God, and while this would be terrifying for any mother, it's something God called her to do so he could have his perfect will accomplished and rescue humanity.

And ultimately, what did this sacrifice do for humanity through suffering? It saved you. It saved me. It has given us the ability to live abundant and sacrificial lives. The pouring out of ourselves will make the broken bits in our lives whole. The pouring out of ourselves is like someone else's frankincense and myrrh; it's a gift to give yourself away so Christ can manifest in you and through you.

So, when the suffering comes and the weeping begins, remember that Christ also wept before his body was crucified. Oh, this is sacrificial love. A beautiful liturgy in Douglas McKelvey's *Every Moment Holy* reads:

Is it possible
that when we weep and don't know why,
it is because the curse has ranged
so far, so wide? That we weep at that
which breaks your heart, because it
has also broken ours—sometimes so deeply
that we cannot explain our weeping,
even to ourselves?
If that is true,
then let such weeping be received, O Lord,
as an intercession newly forged of holy sorrow.
Then let our tears anoint these broken things,
and let our grief be as their consecration—
a preparation for their promised
redemption, our sorrow sealing them
for that day when you will take
the ache of all creation,
and turn it inside-out,
like the shedding of
an old gardener's glove.

This liturgy spoke to my mental brokenness amidst motherhood and marriage. It spoke to the sorrow in my spirit. Sometimes I wonder if it will ever fade away, but then I remember
that God anguished.

Is it possible that you—in your sadness
over Lazarus, in your grieving for
Jerusalem, in your sorrow in the garden—
is it possible that you have sanctified
our weeping too?[9]

It's only possible through a holy and righteous God to sanctify anguish and pain; the world will not bring healing, and the world will worsen. The word *sanctify* means to set apart as or to declare holy; consecrate. Psalm 56:8 reads: "Record my misery; list my tears on your scroll—are they not in your record?" It means your tears are not discounted from dissension with your spouse or a dull day of deep depression. Motherhood is sacrificial because the giving of ourselves is the sacrifice of our energy, time, emotions, and wants. We're not concerned with ourselves when our babies throw up, can't sleep, or wail in the market aisle. We're concerned for their well-being, their safety, and their lives. Our holiness is not centered on ourselves. Our holiness is a striving to be more Christ-like. By acknowledging this holiness, we are equipped to share it throughout motherhood; when our babes wail or fuss or tantrum themselves to the ends of the world, we can bear it because Christ already took it all.

He even bore the day I could take no more.

The day ended as any ordinary day until something in me was triggered by a word Omar used. I thought this part of my story was over, but it wasn't. This goes to say that motherhood does not fix our woes. Motherhood is not a cure-all.

We haven't suddenly arrived because we've become mothers, which, in essence, is idolizing motherhood. Motherhood, for me at least, is something I needed to grow into and grow with. After all, Elias was only one and a half when it became too much to bear.

I yelled obscenities at my husband, ran upstairs, and locked myself in a room. I cried until I couldn't anymore. I looked around and saw the razor-sharp accessories I use to scrape oil paint. The scissors lay beside them. Heaving, I grabbed them and sat against the wall, the room warm. Then, satisfied and bleeding, everything suddenly enveloped me, and I started weeping. I wept for a long time.

How can I be so broken when my son sleeps peacefully in his crib and my husband is downstairs? How can I be so broken when I have my greatest earthly gifts?

I didn't have an answer. But I know I caressed my pregnant belly that held our daughter with my now bloodied wrist. I shuddered in shame and regret. I sighed, thinking how perhaps I'd taken a million steps backward after all my progress.

I didn't tell Omar until days later why I had bandaged my wrist. He was so bereaved when I told him; he held me close and rocked me in his arms. With his encouragement, I sought weekly counseling and have been going ever since. Seeking out the help I need has slowly moved me forward to change my warped view of myself and the world.

Not everyone is out to get me.

Not everyone is out to get *you*.

Not everyone is against me.

Not everyone hates me for no good reason.

People are rooting for me.

People aren't thinking the worst of me all the time.

It's OK to believe in yourself, too.

It's through the seeking that we begin the healing. And I was all here for it. In this seeking, I also sought God's Word and have genuinely found rest in it. Reading the Bible somehow makes folding laundry feel honorable, as though tending the small things of the home is still part of the ministry of motherhood.

God reminds me that the dirty dishes mean stomachs are full, a messy tub means my son has enjoyed bath time and rubber ducks, and a toy-littered floor means toys have been played with, and I welcome it. I almost savor the mess sometimes because I know it won't always be this way; I know I'll have a Cheerio-less floor one day and I'll miss hearing my children's feet shuffle across the floor.

I treasure these moments with my children; I delight in them because I know every day is a gift. I know my son's tiny hand that touches the stairwell while I carry him up will one day help him down the stairs as a grown boy. I know my son's babbling will become a powerful voice one day. I know they will one day be world changers, even if it looks like motherhood or fatherhood or being a missionary or a writer or even a doctor. Whatever they delight in that honors God will slowly change the world.

When Emmanuel gives good gifts to us out of his mercy, the outpouring of our immense adoration of God gives it all back. We give it back because we know we don't deserve it. So how do I give it back? I try to steward my motherhood well and to the utmost glory of Christ Jesus. I'll never forget the day my husband whispered with wet cheeks, "We need to be like the elders who just cast their crowns at the feet of Jesus because we know it's not ours, nothing is ours, it's all his." And then my husband wept in humbleness, and all I could do was stroke his face and agree in love.

Living given in motherhood is like having the heart of Abraham, who was going to sacrifice his one and only beloved son, Isaac, his inheritance and heritage. It's fearing the Lord in reverence and obedience. It's not because we know we'll see the ram caught in the thicket by its horns, but because we trust all to Jesus.

> The angel of the Lord called to Abraham from heaven a second time and said, "I swear by myself, declares the Lord, that because you have done this and have not withheld your son, your only son, I will surely bless you and make your descendants as numerous as the stars in the sky and as the sand on the seashore. Your descendants will take possession of the cities of their enemies, and through your offspring all nations on earth will be blessed, because you have obeyed me. (Gen. 22:15-18)

It's easy to disregard this blessing of inheritance when you have dishes to do or loads of laundry to fold up, but when your children's eyes widen with joy while being tickled or chased, you can't help but cherish the inheritance of your babies. They are a joy. They are a blessing. They are our heritage, too.

I know the future is a long journey. My children will grow up, and we'll have seasons of despair and hardship, but motherhood also displays the cross shape in our own lives to our children. So how do we take the form of the cross to show Christ's glory in us?

When we think our children are not living up to our standards, we embody grace and love them well through it. When we feel our children are purposefully acting out in rebellion against us, we draw them closer and show them the exuberant love of Christ. When we believe our children, in given seasons, don't love us, we love them anyway. Why do we do this? Because we are mothers striving to show Christ's love to our children, just as we are trying to show Christ's love to our spouses. We are caretakers. We desire God's will above anything.

When the candles are blown out on the farm table and the dishes are all put away, did we love our children well when they accidentally dropped the glass plate? Did we crouch low and tell them that it was an accident and everything would be OK? When the humdrum of the day has quieted, and our children are arguing in the bathroom upstairs, did we teach them to disagree well, or did we yell in frustration out of our tiredness? When the days grow dark and the stars settle in the sky, did we, as mothers, honor God with how we loved our children that day?

I know I won't get it perfect; it won't be easy. I know there will be times when parenting will be as messy as the first time my baby ate spaghetti, but I also know there is enough grace God gives me to pour out sacrificially; there is enough from his harvest for us all to yield from.

This is what I desire to do for my children; I want them to know I tried daily to sacrifice myself for them. I want them to know I was a gracious, patient mother. I want them to come to me and be able to whisper in my ear, "Hey, mama, that wasn't nice." I want my children to be able to approach me in love.

I also want them to know amidst parenting and discipline what my hands enjoy doing most: baking sugar cookies and flooding them with homemade royal icing and hearing my son crunch on a green dinosaur cookie, hearing my daughter coo on her tummy, or simply holding them and swaying in their rocking chair, feeling their little bodies wrapped in my arms.

My children won't grapple with how their mama pushes through depression, but my husband will. Our children will see how I treat Omar and how he treats me.

At times, they may hear the breaking of my voice towards my husband or the frustration of my husband towards me, and even towards them at times; more than anything, they will learn to embody a sacrificial love because it's a sacrificial love they will see in me and our home. This is my *sacred burden*; I'm here for it. I'm here to grow. I'm here to grow into a more gracious and tender wife and mother. At the same time, though, I knew I needed to talk to my doctor. So, with the assurance from my psychiatrist, I started back up on medication. By the end of 2021, I had my antidepressant dose increased.

Nine

Regression

Let mothers labor to make home the happiest place in the world.
Charles Spurgeon

We are nearing winter as November 2021 comes to a close; the leaves are dying, and even the fields are resting. Every year, this season reminds me of God's goodness in allowing me to close in on another year of life. I'm reminded that old things break and die to themselves to give birth to the new, as much as Jesus Christ did for us on that rugged cross. It reminds me, almost pulls me, to draw closer to Jesus Christ as he draws closer to me. All of it makes me wonder about beholding the wonder. Mary and Joseph saw the face of God in a manger, the gifts of the wise men who traveled by star, and the gift that God gave that beautiful night in Bethlehem.

Mary gave birth to the Son of Man, and I wonder just how awestruck she was as she looked down upon the face of the Savior. Here I am, centuries later, holding my son in my arms, his big brown eyes full of wonder. My hands gather over my 37-week pregnant belly, knowing she'd be here soon.

To say our home was a carousel of joy during my last trimester carrying Analia would be a lie. I was swollen, my feet looked like pink pig's feet, my stomach was in constant dire pain, and my white bedsheets were always pressed in with my heavy, pregnant body. Of course, I pushed through the pain, but mentally, I was ready for her to be here in every way.

Our faux pine tree was already decorated, and our front porch's lambency lit the darkness. I remember coming home from the grocery store and my husband hanging the last wobbly Christmas lights to make me smile after a grody pregnant day. I shuffled up the stairs with our son to lull him to nap. After gazing at him in his crib, I wondered about the kind of older brother he'd be. I started smiling, thinking about him protecting Analia, building sandcastles together, or giving her kisses on the forehead.

You're going to be the best big brother, my Elias Luke.

It was the second day of Advent, December 2nd, 2021. I started working on her unfinished room, and by evening, it was finished; pictures and paintings hung, covers fitted, and animals sat. It looked beautiful, and I started to tear up. I couldn't wait to surprise Omar when he got home from the hospital.

"We're ready for you, darling girl," I whispered while looking about the room.

At 2:30 a.m. on December 3rd, my stomach grew tight. I winced. Once it went away, it happened again about five minutes later. I started counting, as my husband always encouraged me to do. After the pain grew worse, I woke him.

"Omar, I'm in pain," I heaved. "I think I'm having contractions." Then, I heard him roll over under our sheets.

"Are they growing worse? How far apart are they?"

After I told him, he checked to see how dilated I was.

"Oh, I am always getting an epidural!" I shouted. Meanwhile, our poor cat, Mia, was growling at Omar, not understanding that he was doing a cervical exam. We both laughed at the cat.

"You're four centimeters dilated." I heard the lilt in his voice.

"Oh, my goodness. Really?" I started breathing heavily while another contraction began. I quickly got dressed and ready in the bathroom. Omar grabbed our bags, picked up our sleeping son from his crib, and by 3 a.m., we were out the door.

By 12:30 p.m. on December 3rd, our Analia Lucy was born; I was 37 weeks and six days pregnant. As I was pushing, Omar said my belly looked like a giant balloon. Gratitude rushed into me as he placed her on my chest and later cut the umbilical cord. My girl babe wrapped in vernix, placed on my naked chest, already had a whole place in my heart to love deeply.

Things will be different this time around, my darling girl. I thought as she nursed on me. In every way, things will be different. They were by the grace of God that met me where I was. I didn't suffer from PPD as I had with my dear boy when he was born. My colostrum came in, and she was able to nurse. My milk came in a few days later, and breastfeeding has been a blessing.

In the coming months, Elias would giggle and kiss her forehead every time I stooped to sweep her gently against his face. I felt like I was living in a miracle; everything was going well. And so, I was lowered to 50 mg of my anti-depressant, having needed 150 mg while pregnant. Of course, this reduction is not an excuse for my outbursts, as it is never OK, but there was a noticeable difference in my mood when Analia turned about five months.

I suddenly felt a regression. It was like I had rewound time. My husband came in with our toddler from a morning run, and Elias started fussing.

"Did you feed him?" My voice was harsh.

"Why do you talk to me like that?" he asked. "I can tell you're already on edge because I went running with him, and he hasn't eaten yet."

"Well, every morning, I feed him. He's crying right now because he's hungry."

"No, he's crying because he's scared of you."

"Don't even start, Omar," I fumed. I pushed my plate from me. "Do you really want to do this right now?"

"I want respect, Samantha. That's all I'm asking—"

"No, you want a saint. You're controlling and rude and can't wait to call me out when I do something wrong. Well, go and find that perfect saint and let me know when you find her. I'm starting to resent you," I yelled.

Elias's face scrunched, and he started crying behind Omar, reaching up for him.

"The only resenting that will end up happening is our kids resenting you if you continue to act this way," he retorted.

My heart lurched in anger. "Don't you ever say that!" I got up. "Don't you dare talk about my kids' emotions."

"Our kids—"

"You know what, from here on out, I'm not talking to you," I grabbed my phone and pretended to be on it, ignoring him.

"The irony is that you're mad at me," he said.

I couldn't contain it. I grabbed Analia's jar of pureed rolled oats, banana, and pumpkin and thrust it to the floor. The glass shattered everywhere, and the remaining puree splattered on the floor, resembling bird dung on a windshield. Everyone grew silent, including Elias. His glassy eyes looked up at me.

Omar took Elias to his playroom, and I was left alone with a cooing Analia, regretting what I had done. I looked at the mess on the floor, the shards of glass reminding me of what I had worked so hard to overcome. I sighed, got up, and grabbed the broom and dustpan. As I swept, I breathed heavily in and out, wondering why I got to that breaking point.

Why am I constantly sweeping up my broken mess?

I heard Elias saying colors to Omar.

"Blue!" he started giggling while I heard scribbling on the play table. Then I listened to his little feet near the kitchen where the mess was. They both came out quickly.

"No, Elias. Quédate aquí," Omar said as he took Elias in his arms. They both sat down at the farm table. After sweeping, I went to them and sat on the wooden slab, my feet dangling like a little girl's feet on a bench.

"I'm sorry," I whispered, my face contorted and my body bent over. "I love you, Omar."

"I love you, and I forgive you, my love," Omar gently placed our boy on the floor and gathered me in his arms. He swept my face tenderly, "We are called to be holy; you know this. Christ has given you a new heart. Don't forget that, my love," he said.

"You don't think I've gotten better?" I retorted.

"Yes, you have, and I'm so grateful for that. Our son's tantrums are like yours. He can't healthily express his emotions, just like you can't when you go into a tantrum. But you're a new creation in Christ, and we don't have to live by the flesh anymore," he said. I sighed and hugged him tightly while our son grabbed onto my legs.

During this moment, I had a long morning of wondering how in the world I got to that point again. At the same time, though, I reflected on how my former self would have gone the whole day in a broken state, but that morning, I chose to walk toward forgiveness. Instead of wallowing in my misery of feeling like a busted sinner, I could change the story of that day.

By God's grace, you can also change the motif of your story. Instead of the narrative of sin following offense, we should make room for forgiveness and humility to fill the story. Instead of sin following sorrow, we should make room for hope and meditation on God's Word (Matt 6:32). While we're dealing with mental illness, whichever diagnosis, changing the recurring theme of our stories is difficult but not impossible. When we have submitted our lives to Jesus Christ, we are indeed a new creation (2 Cor. 5:17); thus, doing the impossible will be possible through Christ. It is nothing we can do of our own accord: "All of us have become like one who is unclean, and all our righteous acts are like filthy rags; we all shrivel up like a leaf, and like the wind, our sins sweep us away" (Isaiah 64:6).

Imagine someone who has had several miscarriages for unknown reasons, but one day, she finds out she's pregnant again and giddily tells her husband and doctor. She is joyous. She is hopeful. She believes things will be different this time, only a week later, to have passed the baby painfully. Anyone's insides would naturally curl in sorrow for this person as they experience, yet again, another loss. (My husband says a certain amount of miscarriages are related to unknown causes.) I still can't grapple with this: how can a person who loves the Lord have to endure such loss? I was reminded of this verse in Romans 8:22-28:

> We know that the whole creation has been groaning as in the pains of childbirth right up to the present time. Not only so, but we ourselves, who have the first fruits of the Spirit, groan inwardly as we wait eagerly for our adoption to sonship, the redemption of our bodies. For in this hope we were saved. But hope that is seen is no hope at all. Who

hopes for what they already have? But if we hope for what we do not yet have, we wait for it patiently.

In the same way, the Spirit helps us in our weakness. We do not know what we ought to pray for, but the Spirit himself intercedes for us through wordless groans. And he who searches our hearts knows the mind of the Spirit, because the Spirit intercedes for God's people in accordance with the will of God. And we know that in all things God works for the good of those who love him, who have been called according to his purpose.

It's hard to grapple with the idea that miscarriages are a part of the Lord's will, but all we can do is trust him that he is working all things out for our good and his glory. As we groan for children, he groans for his children. While we are expectant for the things of the world, whether a spouse, children, or something else, let's not forget that we are awaiting the redemption of our bodies, too. Our bodies fail us: cancer looms, miscarriages occur, diseases spread, brain tumors form, and our bodies constantly fight infections. Yet, even through the breaking of our bodies, we can still utter a benediction.

God designed our bodies in the most sacred disposition, for the most sacred reason—to glorify him. Even when our bodies fail, our Great Physician is not taken aback by it— he comes close to us and weeps with us. Just like he would have for our church friend who miscarried again. I remember standing beside her as she thanked Omar for "truly caring about your patients." It swelled my heart with even more love for my husband because I know he works to serve God and to meet people where they are. "It has been said that a minister sees men and women at their best; a lawyer sees them at their worst; and a doctor sees them as they are."[10]

William Barclay's commentary on the book of Luke opened my eyes to the heart of the Gentile doctor and how he yearned to write the narrative of the Savior in a personable way.

This is what Jesus Christ does for us; he meets us right where we are. For me, he met me in my indisposition of depression and traits of BPD. Through the spurring of my gentle husband, I was able to not only seek help but realize that Christ gave me a new heart (Ezek. 36:26), a renewed mind (Eph. 4:23), and is ultimately bringing me from glory to glory until the day I am called home (2 Cor. 4:16).

I remember when we were pregnant with our daughter, and we went to do a sonogram around 17 weeks, I saw her body's grainy movement, her features showing, and her little legs kicking. I felt my insides fill with joy and fear. Will I be a good mother? Will she love me as her mother? What will she say of me when she's old enough to talk? I started growing fears, as many of us mothers do, but then I realized that I needed to not only renew my mind in Christ but renew my mind in how I perceived my motherhood journey battling mental illness.

Depression will tell me I'm a horrible mother; it will make me feel inadequate and bring me unreasonable guilt. Depression will whisper lies that I'm not equipped for this and am ill-suited for motherhood. In reality, my striving to be a holy mother is for the glory of Christ Jesus first, not for my husband or even my children, but it's in the outpouring of my seeking to glorify God that I can serve my family well. Granted, I will sometimes fail, but his mercy and grace are new every morning (Lam. 3:22-24). This is good news for someone who fails quite a bit.

Moreover, as I sought to be the mother God called me to be, it had me reflect on his good and holy nature in motherhood. God is gracious, hopeful, loving, patient, and sacrificial. These are truths he would show me in not only marriage but motherhood.

Soon, my son will be two-years-old. I get emotional just thinking about my children growing up. Omar can attest that I may be overly emotional when Elias does something new, like saying a new word or understanding how to blow kisses. Sometimes, I watch him *ROAR* like a lion, chase our cat, and think how blessed I am to be his mother. I get to hold him close to my chest. I feel his small lips pressed against my cheek, giving me a *beso*. As I watched our son playing with his cars on the wooden floor, saying *VROOM VROOM*, I was sweetly reminded of how innocent he is. He's a sweet, Crayon-loving boy who loves bright balls, stuffed zoo animals, and cuddling his little sister. He doesn't know anything about suffering quite yet, and my motherly heart wishes with everything in me that I could protect my children from it—but it will come, and there's nothing I can do to stop the suffering from coming. All I can do is somehow prepare them better for it. The only way I know how to do that is to share Jesus Christ with them, to stoop and whisper Jesus loves you every night in their innocent ears. Jesus didn't come to eradicate suffering but to be with us in it; he bends toward us and whispers in our ears I am here for you. I am with you in this.

Suffering produces perseverance, and for those suffering from the mind, sometimes, that's all we can do. Keep going. Press forward. Hope. Believe. Even if we regress at times, because we will, we can press forward knowing that God simply isn't going anywhere. He is right there with us, anguishing with us. He watches us make messes of things, like the way my son crayons over the door frames, or the way he throws tantrums on the floor, or when he cries in my arms—God watches us tenderly, whispering to our broken hearts, "[I] lift up those who are bowed down...(Ps. 146:8).

We know Jesus was active in his ministry, healing the sick and performing miracles, but let's not forget that he was most concerned about the heart.

He is more invested in our sick hearts having faith than getting healed. It is our coming to faith, renouncing sin, believing in him, and the spurring of this good work that he cares most about. He doesn't want us to regress; he wants us to press forward. "But they did not listen or pay attention; instead, they followed the stubborn inclinations of their evil hearts. They went backward and not forward" (Jer. 7:24).

We must do the hard and holy work of pressing forward and not giving up. Still, we must also remember the grace of God that meets us where we are, whether we're on the floor weeping in a puddle of tears or reading to our toddler after a homemade breakfast, hearing him QUACK like a duck in a puddle.

God is ever with us in *both* circumstances.

Ten

The Right Plane

It is not the healthy who need a doctor, but the sick.
Jesus, *Matthew 9:12*

I remember waking early one morning to feed my daughter. Afterward, I cooked breakfast for my son and me and set him in his playroom so I could do the dishes. It always worked.

Around lunchtime, I did the same, only to return to find my two-year-old in his poop smeared all over the floor with tracings all over his toys. It was on his baseball bat, on the wall, and even in his fingernails. I gasped and stared at him for a while. His eyes looked up at me while his body sat surrounded by poop as though sitting surrounded by his Crayons. He didn't know. I picked him up and went to the bathroom to put him in the shower, and he grew so afraid and started to cling to me, poop-smeared fingers and all. With poop on my pants, I cradled him to my chest and said, "It's OK, baby. It's OK. Mama's here."

While he was crying, my daughter started wailing. I called Omar telling him that I needed help. I didn't have fresh milk for Analia then, so I had to pump.

When my husband finally came home, the first thing he said was, "This is why we don't—"

I yelled. I cursed. I ran upstairs to feed our daughter. He came in with our boy on his hip, and I yelled at my husband to get out and how I was fine without him. Elias started crying; this is one of those things I lament; his crinkled face in fear with his big brown eyes opened wide.

"You're scaring him, Samantha."

"Get out! It's your fault he's scared for bringing him in here! I was fine without you."

"They're crying because they're scared of you."

"Get out!" I yelled as I cradled my daughter to my chest and tried to rock her in the chair.

"I forgive you," he said as he slipped out the door. I wept over her light brown hair and wished I could erase this evening with everything in me.

Days like this broke me and made me feel like a failure. Yet, God taught both my husband and me that day.

For my husband: not to tend to the mess first. In my hurt, I told him, "You don't go and tend to the poop first. You tend to us." He apologized for saying what he had said and mentioned how he'd tend to our needs first, not the mess. The mess can always wait to be picked up.

For me, instead of blowing up, I should reflect grace and gentleness. While we are getting better with this, we are still not perfect at it, and we fail many days, but we're pointed in the right direction.

Marriage can often get put to the wayside when babes come wrapped in your arms, but the truth is marriage needs to be tended to just like a wee one. It needs nursing, tending, love, sacrifice, and time.

Omar and I worked hard to make sacrifices for one another when our babies came; sometimes, it looked like him carrying a load of dishes for a week, so we could come together at night without me being overly tired. Sometimes, it looked like him cleaning poop off the floor while I bathed our baby girl upstairs. Sometimes, it looked like me putting aside my own free time to spend it with him for a romantic night. Sometimes, it looked like two tired parents reading over coffee and strawberries at 8 p.m., relishing what time we had left that day.

The point is that time is even more sacred when babies come into the picture; despite what that day holds, we always come together at night.

During this season, I reflected on how Christ was always working in me; when I met Omar, I was a different person. I was a homebody, completely secluded, and enjoyed being very much alone. I suspect many of us can agree that it feels somehow safe this way. But, over time, this method would fail. As I grew to love the Father more and Omar more, I realized that as part of his body, I was not meant to live life secluded; I was to live life open and given.

I didn't enjoy socializing. I didn't enjoy even going to Church. Yet through our woes and trials of my depression, I've grown to treasure being an active body member of the Church because it was through this that my depression lessened. Jesus Christ showed me that being around brothers and sisters in Christ was another prescription my heart needed. My husband told me how he noticed this change when we moved to our second home. I love hosting. I love being a host. I love gathering. I love our house being a gathering place. I love when our table is full of laughter and openness. I love when meals are shared and hearts are poured out. This is healing.

Healing is a long journey of letting. It's allowing God to toil your scarred and barren land into becoming. It's not becoming more successful, prettier, popular, or admirable, even—it's becoming more like the One who chases every day after you.

And even when I slam doors shut and throw spoons across the kitchen in anger, God still graciously opens doors and gracefully throws his arms around me. And so, as I now hold both my children in my arms, my son wiggling and squirming and my daughter cooing as six-month-olds do, I'm reminded that God didn't need to bless me with them, or even with my husband, but he chose to.

When Omar comes home from work, he'll tell me the types of surgeries he's had, and if I'm lucky, he'll use white napkins to cut into as show and tell. I always give him the dead eyes because, for some reason, I'll cut napkins in half so they can have a longer shelf life.

He proceeds to tear into the napkin with his fingers: "I'm cutting laterally into the...." His voice trails into something like a song as he continues to complete the surgery, then pulls back and says, "So, there you go."

I stare at him and marvel at how he talks like one of the medical books on our bookshelves. He grins and shrugs humbly.

He came home one day later than usual; he hung up his keys, sat at the table, and sighed.

"Are you OK? What happened?" I asked.

"I had a tough surgery today, my hardest yet."

I placed our dinner on the table, and he told me about it while we ate.

"This surgery had a large fibroid uterus; the difference with this case was that the fibroid was in the bottom part of the uterus and on the cervix." He grabbed a napkin. "So, in essence, it was kind of like an iceberg."

I didn't care about the napkin; I just wanted to hear about his most complex surgery in his ten years of practice.

His patient proved to be his most challenging case, given how large the fibroid was and how it was positioned. Omar told me that the cervix is very complex; one has to figure out the best approach: whether laparoscopically or abdominally with a larger incision or vaginally. Omar initially started this case laparoscopically to get enough visualization around the fibroid, but he couldn't see where the cervix met the vagina, so he tried to look vaginally but could not locate the plane.

Her fibroid was 11cm in size, which is about 4.5in. large. He tells me that a surgeon must absolutely know where the cervix ends laterally on its base and where the vagina connects with it because that's where one makes the cut.

"I ended up having to open this patient, which is the third route—what we call the most invasive route and the one that increases the highest risk for infection." He sighed. "By opening her, though, I could then palpate the fibroid, and I had a sense of where it ended and was able to cut wherever the vagina connected to the cervix."

The challenge with these surgeries is knowing when to stop cutting because one can cut into the vagina or the tubes that drain the kidneys. Or, posteriorly, a surgeon can cut into the rectum, which then a general surgeon would need to be called.

It matters what tools you use, like how the sharp-pointed tips of iris scissors are best suited for precise fistula repairs or how traditional laparoscopic scissors are used to cut sutures.[11] Tools matter in order to get the intended outcome you're looking for.

My husband continued, "There are gentle instruments that pick up ends of a blood vessel, and then there are tough instruments that will grab onto more dense tissue like the fascia. If you use the wrong tool, you risk injuring the patient."

And just like a doctor mustn't use the wrong surgical equipment during surgeries, so members of Christ's body shouldn't use the wrong tools to help one another heal.

I believe we all need healing in one form or another, whether from a breaking of the mind, the skin, or something that's internally breaking our hearts apart. For those suffering from the breaking of the mind, we need someone to hear us. We need someone to love us through our manic episodes and out-of-control emotions. We need stability. We need a dependable sort to come alongside our undependable mind, someone who has the likeness of the heart of Christ, to spur us into the arms of Christ when our bodies fail us or when we're in the thick of it all.

I was Omar's hardest case to date; our marriage was his hardest surgery. He didn't use the right tools at first: trying to hold me down, taking away my keys, hiding liquor, tracking me, calling me a child, and often raising his voice. After several months, he realized none of these routes were working to help treat what was happening inside me. When we fought, it was either serious or something utterly silly. When I got offended, I often carried pain deep inside me that exuded wrath; for Omar, he often retreated. Yet, when these fights happened, I noticed the very things coming out of my mouth could not be any more unrelated to what I was truly anguishing over inside. I was carrying pails of pain, and it mattered what words he said, the words that triggered me to lose myself in seconds. So it is with someone getting performed on; of course, the doctor doesn't want to cause more harm to an already "diseased" area; he wants to bring healing by using the correct instruments.

My husband was not cutting through fresh tissue with me; he was cutting through layers of scars. As he's told me, this makes surgeries harder to perform.

"In terms of doing surgery, you have to find what's called the right plane," he said. "This means finding the normal tissue, cutting through the scar tissue, and separating it out until you find the normal plane. Ah, now the anatomy is restored. Now I can see clearly, and that's something I do every time I do surgery."

Maybe one is scarred from life, childhood, parents, abusers, accusers, or the Church. It takes time to heal from these pains; it takes time for healing to come about in the first place, let alone knowing where to start. When God brought my doctor-husband into my life, he knew this man would aid me in healing, the slow process of sanctifying my broken mind. By the spurring of my husband, I now seek help for my mental illness. These tools have helped cut through the scar tissue so that true healing can take place—*so one can see the right plane.*

"For example, as you're cutting through tissue to do a hysterectomy," he continued. "You want to be sure you can see around the tissue, so you're not cutting intestine or tubes that drain the kidney or a blood supply to the ovary. If you don't do that, you're going to be reckless, and you're apt to hurt a patient."

We need others to help us cut through the scar tissue to bring true healing. We cannot self-perform these surgeries. We need to trust those equipped to help us.

The surgery of the heart is never done; the Great Physician is always working on it until he calls us home. Then, however, the pruning takes place with his surgical hands. The Great Surgeon knows what he's doing; he uses precision and deep cuts because he is a God all too familiar with scar tissue in his perforated hands and feet and what resulted from that deep cut.

He knows that if we trust his hands to perform the surgeries on our broken hearts, we will be able to trust him through it; we will be able to have hope through it and peace in it.

There is an insurmountable joy when we rise from that hospital bed into the laying down of ourselves before him, who brings the healing. There is no better place to be. The abundant life of healing, restoration, and joys that are to be revealed when we accept this process is inconceivable.

It doesn't seem possible to have joy when you're throwing a lamp across the room, but there is when your husband somehow makes you laugh through the blackening of the room. We've done this laughing game many times; I'll tell my husband through tears and chuckles, "I'm not laughing right now. I'm very upset." My husband smiles and draws me close to his chest.

"Why are you so wonderful to me?" I cry.

"Because I love you, and we're a team," he smiles.

My sweet balm of healing.

Granted, it will less often look like this and be more of this: through the weeping of tears, through the uplifting words of your family, through friends showing up, through counseling and mentorship, through the blessed joys of motherhood for those of us who are mamas, and through your spouse showing gracious love to you while you're in the thicket of darkness.

It may take longer for some than others, given the amount of scar tissue one has. The healing process will come to those willing to accept God's grace and healing versus those wallowing in the same pain, believing no one else truly gets it. Perhaps, you think not a single doctor can truly diagnose the problem you seem to have.

God already knows your diagnosis, and he already knows your cure. God gets your pain. His hands, feet, and once-broken heart prove this. We need to trust the Great Surgeon with the surgery of our hearts.

"Many times, we're just chopping stuff, and we're fighting each other in our marriage and hurting these other structures," my husband said over his blueberry cobbler.

"We need to see the right plane to know where to cut," I whispered, taking his hand.

Afterword

For me, today, I'm pushing through the feeling of dereal-ization to be present with my son while we bake sugar cookies. This is the fruit of living in thanksgiving, *joy*, even amidst the unfeeling. I will choose, day by day, to give my husband and children that which is *from the harvest before me*, not the scraps mental illness tells me I have left to give.

Don't wait for the miracle, as though one day you'll wake up depression-free. Instead, take the time to cultivate your roots in The Word of *God* and be near to him. Glean from his harvest, friend. He is enough for you and has a never-ending supply.

So, why don't we do something together? Let's pray this out loud:

Father of all anguishes, who wept for us—we come before you full of our brokenness, asking for you to stretch out your hand to be nearer to us. Above all things in this wretched world, we seek you and want you above even the ghastly desire to be rid of this depres-sion—this illness. May our wanting for you be our open cry because you are the God who is close to the broken-hearted. We ask, Elohim, to cultivate in us the harvest you know is here—Lord, speak to our bruised spirits just long enough so we can run with your sweet truths through these fields of glory. We know a grain of wheat must break and die to produce fruit, and in the same way, may the breaking of ourselves be the harvest—because the harvest is you. In Christ's holy name, Amen.

If you come from a broken past of abuse and trauma, I pray that you break generational curses off of you and for your children. Be strongly rooted in the One who died to break these brittle chains of trauma off of you and who rose again to raise you up from the dead with him. You were not born to remain dead in your sins, but to accept Jesus Christ as your Lord and Savior to commune with the Holy One who set you free from *all of it*. In so doing, you break the yoke off your back because you now realize you don't need to carry it because Jesus has already carried it for you, up that hill to the top of Calvary on that one wooden cross.

While breaking that yoke off, you can now jubilantly break bread on your table from the harvest of your one life lived surrendered to the Father because he gave you the harvest of harvests. He gave you his son. God will never run out of himself, and we will never be able to outrun the Father. This is good news for us who like to run away when things get hard.

So, while I'm breaking bread on my own wooden farm table with my two-year-old saying *sau-se* for his sausage and my eight-month-old daughter cooing, I can thank God who blessed me with a life I could never have dreamed. I give thanks and live given because I want to reflect that sacrificial love to my family the way Christ loved me through my own brokenness and sin. So, like a pitcher, Lord, pour me out like a living sacrifice because it is in this way, through the bending of myself to pick up smooshed *sau-ses* off the floor, that I am fulfilling my calling.

I remember one ordinary Sunday after church, Omar and I were talking in our room while the babies napped. He surprised me by taking my hands in his.

"Are your scars still there?" He turned over my left arm and traced my wrist gently.

"Yes, they are," he said while he looked at me with a soft smile. "I'm glad. It's a reminder of how far God has taken you —how far he has taken *us*."

Chapter Discussion Questions

Imagine yourself as a living house. God comes in to rebuild that house. At first, perhaps, you can understand what He is doing. He is getting the drains right and stopping the leaks in the roof and so on; you knew that those jobs needed doing and so you are not surprised. But presently He starts knocking the house about in a way that hurts abominably and does not seem to make any sense. What on earth is He up to? The explanation is that He is building quite a different house from the one you thought of – throwing out a new wing here, putting on an extra floor there, running up towers, making courtyards. You thought you were being made into a decent little cottage: but He is building a palace. He intends to come and live in it Himself.

C.S. Lewis

(Not all of these questions are applicable to everyone, so please feel welcome to discuss or journal the ones that apply more directly to you.)

Chapter One Questions

1. What do you turn to in response to your depression and anguish?
2. How do you react to your spouse when you feel despondent?
3. Where do you find hope?

Chapter Two Questions

1. If you have been diagnosed with a mental disorder/s, feel welcome to list them here:
2. What things have you found yourself running away from —physically, mentally, emotionally, or spiritually?
3. How do you find yourself coping with your mental illness?
4. How has your spouse helped you through your mental sickness if you are married?

Chapter Three Questions

1. How have you denied your brokenness?
2. Do you feel the need to justify your pain, and how do you think that is reflected in your marriage?
3. Do you wholly believe that the death of Christ was for all your brokenness, including what you haven't yet experienced?

Chapter Four Questions

1. What are you feeling most hopeless about?
2. Does your spouse show you more sacrificial love or judgment?
3. I encourage you to speak about what hurts you and see how you can come together over it.

Chapter Five Questions

1. How has your spouse been sharpening you towards the likeness of Christ?
2. How is God using your marriage to purify and sanctify you day by day?
3. I encourage you to remember that God brought you both together and to not let your brokenness or his brokenness separate you (Mark 10:9).

Chapter Six Questions

1. How did you, if so, suffer from depression after your pregnancy?
2. What was unexpected about the first few weeks or months of motherhood?
3. In what ways did you commune with God during this season?

Chapter Seven Questions

1. What changes did you make to push through depression?
2. How did slowing down, if so, help you refocus things in your life?
3. How do you find that God lavishes grace upon you through your depression?

Chapter Eight Questions

1. In what specific ways do you find yourself sacrificing for your children and family?
2. Does the mundane of motherhood ever excite you, and if so, what parts do?
3. Do you feel yourself dying more to yourself to live given in motherhood?

Chapter Nine Questions

1. Have you ever experienced a regression?
2. If so, what was your experience like, and how did you overcome your regression?
3. How are your growing spiritually, emotionally, and mentally?

Chapter Ten Questions

1. How is God working through your scar tissue? Is he using your spouse to aid in the process of healing?
2. How are you finding healing through your mental illness?
3. If after all of this, and through the finishing of this book, how would you say God is using your scar tissue or mental illness for his glory story in *you*?

Samantha Cabrera graduated from the University of Mary Hardin-Baylor with her BA in Mass Communications/Journalism in 2013. She minored in studio art. Before graduating, she began writing for magazines and other faith-based websites in college. She then moved to California and pursued her MA in English while working on staff at the university newspaper. A year and a half into her program, she transferred to pursue her Master of Fine Arts in Writing from Lindenwood University, where she graduated in 2017. Samantha has written for *Christian Mingle*'s Believe.com for five years as a paid contributing writer and *Faithlife Women*, a division of Logos Bible Software. She has been published in *Christian Woman, Thryve, Niche, Agave, Black Barn Gallery*, and the *Santa Fe Literary Review*, among others; she has over 100 articles on various online Christian websites and magazines. She has also contributed chapters and forwards to published devotionals for women. She is also the founder and editor of *Calla Press*. She is a writer, artist, and certified (7-12) English teacher living in the Texas countryside with her loving husband and their children, Elias and Analia. Glorifying God through storytelling and creativity is her passion. She is a strong advocate for mental illness to become a normal conversation in the Christian Church. She can be found @samanthacabrerastudio. An excerpt from her memoir, *The Doctor's Wife: Battling Mental Illness through Marriage and Motherhood*, won an honorable mention at the WriterCon 2021 contest. This is her first book.

www.samanthacabrerastudio.com

Instagram @samanthacabrerastudio

Published by *Calla Press*

www.callapress.com

Notes

Chapter One

1 E. Van Winkle, The toxic mind: the biology of mental illness and violence, Medical Hypotheses, Volume 54, Issue 1, 2000, Pages 146-156, ISSN 0306-9877, https://doi.org/10.1054/mehy.1998.0834. (https://www.sciencedirect.com/science/article/pii/S0306987798908349)

Chapter Two

2 Robinson, Marilynne. Gilead. Torino: Einaudi, 2017.

3 (Louba) Ben-Noun, Liubov. "What Was the Mental Disease That Afflicted King Saul?" *Clinical Case Studies* 2, no. 4 (October 2003): 270–82. https://doi.org/10.1177/1534650103256296.

Chapter Four

4 Weems, Ann. "Lament Psalm Forty-seven." Poem. In *Psalms of Lament*, 105–6. Louisville, KY: Westminster John Knox Press, 1999.

Chapter Five

5 McKelvey, Douglas Kaine. "A Liturgy for Husband & Wife at Close of Day." Liturgy. In *Every Moment Holy*, 147–50. Nashville, TN: Rabbit Room Press, 2019.

6 Elliot, Elisabeth. A Path Through Suffering. United States: Baker Publishing Group, 2003.

Chapter Six

7 Paula Duarte-Guterman, Benedetta Leuner, Liisa A.M. Galea, The long and short term effects of motherhood on the brain, Frontiers in Neuroendocrinology, Volume 53, 2019, 100740, ISSN 0091-3022, https://doi.org/10.1016/j.yfrne.2019.02.004. (https://www.sciencedirect.com/science/article/pii/S0091302218301237)

8 McBain, Robert D.. Depression, Where Is Your Sting?. United States: Resource Publications, 2021.

Chapter Eight

9 McKelvey, Douglas Kaine. "A Liturgy for Those Who Weep Without Knowing Why." Liturgy. In *Every Moment Holy*, 242-46. Nashville, TN: Rabbit Room Press, 2019.

Chapter Nine

10 Barclay, William. The Gospel of Luke. United States: Westminster John Knox Press, 2001.

Chapter Ten

11 Rogers, Rebecca G. "Clinical and Quality of Life Evaluation, Stress Urinary Incontinence." Essay. In *Female Pelvic Medicine and Reconstructive Surgery: Clinical Practice and Surgical Atlas*, 83–118. New York: McGraw-Hill, 2013

CPSIA information can be obtained
at www.ICGtesting.com
Printed in the USA
BVHW041355180822
644921BV00006B/486

9 780578 293714